YORKSHIRE LEGENDS

Compiled by David Joy

DALESMAN

First Published in Great Britain 1993 by
Dalesman Publishing Company Limited,
Stable Courtyard, Broughton Hall,
Skipton, North Yorkshire BD23 3AE
Text © 1993 **Dalesman Publishing Company Ltd.**

Cover illustration: **Joanne Harkness**

ISBN **1 85568 067 X**
Typeset by **Lands Services**
Printed by **Lavenham Press**

CONTENTS

INTRODUCTION

THIS collection of Yorkshire legends is largely taken from articles, notes and letters which have appeared in the *Dalesman* over the last half century. It ranges widely over the White Rose county from the Dales to the North York Moors and from Robin Hood country to the edge of Bowland. It includes ghosts and spectral happenings, barguests and boggarts, giant monsters and Arthurian knights.

These stories can be read in several ways. They can be entertaining footnotes to north-country history and topography, to its folk-lore and customs. The legends of a land can illuminate its true history with a light of their own which throws into strong relief aspects of bygone life that might have been unknown or overlooked. Even though they are far-fetched and some distance from the truth, such legends can represent the beliefs and ideals of the community from which they spring. A county which forgets its legendary tales is poor indeed, and this collection serves to remind us of Yorkshire's rich and varied store.

Part 1

Legends from the Dales

DON'T GO LOOKING FOR YORKSHIRE FAIRIES!

HAVE you got fairies at the bottom of your garden? What – you don't even believe in fairies? Wouldn't you clap and cheer for poor Tinkerbell? For some reason, the belief in fairies seems to be dissolving faster than faith in other traditional supernatural figures. Others – witches for instance, or possessors of the "second sight" – find a place either in the archaeological picture or in the modern research into extra-sensory perception, or both. In reality, fairies have as good a claim to serious acceptance as the others. The trouble is that they have suffered even more misrepresentation.

In 1792 the Hon. John Byng, later fifth Viscount Torrington, made a horseback tour of northern England which took him to the Malham district of Craven. Here he visited Gordale Scar, which impressed him deeply, and he examined the nearby waterfall and dell called Janet's

Foss. His guide pointed out "on one side of it a little, snug, dry cave," Byng wrote in his Diary, "which he said 'was once inhabited by fairies – but that now they were quite out of fashion'." Traditional in fact says that the cave was inhabited by Janet or Jennett, who was the "queen of all the fairies of those parts". Byng seems to have been told something of this, for he wrote six charming verses about it called *The Fairies Dance*. The poem began:

> *Little Gennet, Fairy trim,*
> *To the merry Dance leads on*
> *Full of pastime, full of whim,*
> *With her playmate, Oberon!*

There, nearly two hundred years ago, you have the same concept of fairies that was usual in Victorian times and still is usual today: the pretty little creatures interested in nothing but tinkling music and dancing something like *Les Sylphides*.

Morgan le Fay, "King" Arthur's formidable half-sister, was a different kettle of fish altogether. A fairy of that sort would have been a far more likely denizen of the waterfall, pool and cave at Gordale. In the pantomime – that repository of forgotten traditions – there are two fairies. The Fairy Godmother is a beneficient spirit who waves her silver wand and everything goes right. The Wicked Fairy by contrast is a sort of Odile.

Morgan appears mainly in this kind of role, full of treachery towards Arthur. On the other hand the Lady of the Lake is the fairy who gives Arthur his magical sword Excalibur.

Nimue, who was either a handmaiden to the Lady and her successor, or the person herself, trapped Merlin in a cave but continued to aid Arthur. That dell in Gordale with its waterfall, caves (one is behind the foss) and the broad pool, could quite easily be envisaged as the scene of some of these events. Jennet might have been a fairy godmother, or a wicked fairy, or both.

Morgan le Fay, often described as a witch, was also known under the Latin form Fata Morgana. This illustrates the descent of the word "fairy" from the early church's way of naming such figures as "Fates", from the classical goddesses who span the thread of life. But "fairy" as a term, has no roots in popular thought, tradition or mythology. That is why it hardly occurs in Yorkshire.

Anybody might think that apart from the Gordale dell – where, in any case, the direct reference is to Jennet – there never had been any fairy-lore in the Dales. In reality, one must look under the correct names, and then they come peeping out of their dens. The fairy Morgan as a witch, the Gordale fairy as Jennet, show a curious confusion (if it really is a confusion). Jennet, Janet or Jenny, is a name that has a peculiarly close connection with the witch-cult.

At once the fairy begins to lose something of the shape of the graceful

little creature with a star on her fair head and clad in a tutu. Fairies of this sort make only fleeting appearances elsewhere in the Dales. One of them is at Tower Hill, Middleton-in-Teesdale, where they are wont to dance and another of their haunts is a mile or two higher up the valley on the Yorkshire side at Holwick. A Middleton woman is said to have seen one of the fairies – a little girl in a green dress and with red eyes.

Red eyes or ears are a characteristic feature of beings from the Other World in ancient Celtic mythology. Barguest, the black fairy hound, has flaming red eyes. So had a fox which stopped momentarily in my headlights. But I mustn't be a spoilsport.

Another dancing-ground for the fairies is on the summit of Elbolton. This is a striking hill beside the village of Thorpe near Grassington in Wharfedale. The very name Elbolton has a strange sound for a hill. Might the "El" be the same as the first element in those curious phrases "ell-maiden", "ell-folk" and, for that matter, "elves"? If so, the fairies of Thorpe may be of very ancient lineage.

When the Saxons came to Britain, they did not talk about "fairies".

Neither did the Celtic-speaking peoples who were already here. It seems likely that some considerable remnants of the dark-haired, small-statured "Iberian" people, who inhabited Britain before the Celts came, were still here at the coming of the Saxons and that they had a reputation for magic. These were what the Celtic Scots still call the "Little People", and the dark men who must be the New Year first-footers "for luck". The Celts called them the Sidh or Sith. That may have been the Little People's own name for themselves.

It may lie behind some of the placenames that end in "seat", "set" or "side" (commonly derived from Scandinavian sources). Simon's Seat in Wharfedale is said to be the "seat of Simon" – only no such Simon is recorded. Saimh-an-Sith would mean something like "the holy place of the elves". This is no more than conjecture; but "the seat of Simon" is not even that.

Most of the still existing names for the fairies, however, were brought by the Saxons. One of them was Thrush or Thresh. Just above Burnsall, a mile and a-half from Elbolton as the elf flies, is Threshkeld – "Fairy Well". Simon's Seat is a little way to the south-east.

Another common term for a fairy was a hob. This of course, was the inspiration for Professor Tolkien's wonderful "hobbits". Sometimes two fairy-terms became united, as in Hobthrush. It may be thought that this gave rise to the legend of a hob threshing the corn for a farmer, as at Close House, near Skipton. This tradition, however, is too strong and too widespread to be explained away like that. Indeed, it suggests that dark-haired Iberians may have been employed as farm labourers (or even slaves) by Celts and Saxons. Perhaps to thresh was simply what a hob or thrush did. In Farndale, near Helmsley, is a tumulus called Obthrush, and in it lived a fairy said to have been named Hob o' th' Hurst; but the etymologists give a variant of hobthrust as "hobthurst" – clearly the same word.

Another term for a fairy was a hood, or just Hood. Near Thirsk is a conical little outlier of the North York Moors called Hood Hill, traditionally associated with the fairies. Only about half-a-mile away, incidentally, is the source of the Elphin Beck!

Still another fairy name is Robin, often extended as Robin Goodfellow (which seems to imply that he was regarded with great favour). But he might almost have been called Robin Hoodfellow. Many folk-lore specialists believe that Robin Hood was really not so much an outlawed medieval freebooter as a forest fairy. The fairies, incidentally, were, like Robin, expert archers. So were the Iberians. A rebel leader in the Middle Ages might well have assumed the name of Robin Hood. But where the name occurs on the map – attached to such a spot as Robin Hood's well, for instance, on Horse Head Moor between Littondale and Langstrothdale – it is more likely to refer to a fairy.

By the way, upper Langstrothdale is haunted by Jerry of Cam, a headless horse – perhaps looking for its head! So don't go looking for fairies in Yorkshire – you are unlikely to find them. Inquire instead for Hob, Thrush, Hood and Robin. Knock on the door of any hill called Something Seat, and you may be admitted to join the dance.

Guy Ragland Phillips (1972)

WHARFEDALE'S STRID

"that fearful chasm,
How tempting to bestride!
For lordly Wharfe is there pent in
With rocks on either side."

DURING the summer of 1807 a visitor to the beautiful country which surrounds Bolton Abbey stood by the Strid and afterwards penned these lines. They have caught the savage character of this tortured reach of the mighty Wharfe, which is not surprising, for the visitor was William Wordsworth. The poem in which this verse appeared was *The Force of Prayer*; or *The Founding of Bolton Priory*, and herein is related

the curious legend of how a fatal accident at the Strid resulted in the establishment of the Priory nearly 800 years ago. But first of all, what is the Strid, and why has it gathered round itself a cloak of tragedy?

The word itself is derived from *stryth* and refers not to the possibility of striding from one bank of the river to the other at this point, but from the tumultuous rush of the waters. At the Strid the river, in the early manhood of its life, is angered by a channel of massive gritstone rocks which stretches for nearly a quarter of a mile, forming a fantastic channel. Although it is only a few feet wide its depth extends to thirty or more feet and the rocks are worn into cave-like hollows. A long pointed rock slopes down from the bank at the narrowest point, smoothed by the passage of myriad feet. This is the Strid jump, but the majority of the people who stand here have more regard for their safety than to attempt the crossing. The leap required is not unusually long, but the bank is so formed that on landing the athlete can easily lose balance and fall or slip backwards. Such an accident is almost certain to be fatal, as the current will drag the luckless person into the deep undercut recesses of the channel.

It was such an accident half-way through the 12th century which is said to have resulted in the establishment of Bolton Priory. Fourteen years after William Fitz-Duncan had defeated the troops of King Stephen in the battle of Clitheroe, David, King of Scotland, established William in the Honour of "Skipton and Crafna". Lady Romille bore him two sons and three daughters and the elder son was survived by the Boy of Egremond. This youth was the hope of the family. He was very fond of hunting, and the woods at Bolton were rich in all manner of game. One day, with a greyhound at leash, he strode through the woods at a point near the Strid. Anxious to reach the other bank of the river, the Boy of Egremond leapt across the foaming waters as he had probably done many times before. But this day the dog held back, and its master was drawn back into the river and drowned.

When an attendant returned to the mother, Lady Aaliza, with the news of the tragedy, she was heartbroken. At this time monks were in residence at a Priory in nearby Embsay and they were quick to seize on the opportunity to having their premises transferred to Bolton. "What could be a more fitting memorial to the dead boy than a fine new Priory by the banks of the Wharfe?" they pleaded. Lady Aaliza was full of grief and in just the right mood to consider the plan, as the monks had realised.

> *Long, long in darkness did she sit,*
> *And her first words, 'Let there be*
> *In Bolton, on the field of Wharfe,*
> *A stately priory.'*

In 1154 the Priory was transferred from Embsay to the banks of lovely Wharfe at Bolton. It was dissolved in 1540, but the ruins have the nobility of age and a grace which even the ravages of history and the weather have not been able to remove. Many historians have not accepted the human ingredient of its foundation; but on a summer's day, when the sunlight slants down on the old ruins and through a canopy of leaves above the Strid, it is difficult not to believe the old story. Much better to ponder upon it than another and less romantic reason why the monks should leave Embsay for Bolton – the wild extremity of the former spot, which the churchmen did not particularly enjoy.

The Rev. Thomas Parkinson has recorded a tradition connected with the Strid, that on the morning of the May-day preceding any fatal accident in the Wharfe a spectral white horse, the steed of the queen of the fairies, is to be seen arising from the spray and mist around the Strid. J. H. Dixon, in his *Chronicles and Stories of the Craven Dales*, takes up this theme. "Can the White Horse of the Strid have any connection with Sliepner the steed of Odin, and is it his mission to convey the spirits of the drowned to the halls of Valhalla?" he asks. Dixon adds: "The White Horse of the Strid may, however, have another origin, and particularly as he is connected with death. He may be the White Horse of the Apocalyptic vision."

A curious tale recorded by A. W. Millar is set in the early years of the 16th century. Living in the vicinity of Bolton were the Tracey family, a good yeoman stock, and they had an only daughter called Gladys, who by all accounts has beautiful and brunette. When she was 18 years of age she fell in the Wharfe and her cries for help were answered by a monk from the Priory, Father Ambrose. He is described as of pleasant countenance, fine physique and about 40 years of age. He jumped into the river, which was running unusually high for summer, and with little difficulty brought the girl to the bank. She was unconscious, but quickly came round. The two forged links of attraction, but Father Ambrose, instead of having his resolve weakened by Gladys at first had his zeal fired for his calling. He was only human and found that he loved the girl, but he betrayed nothing of his inner consciousness when he met her.

Eventually love conquered and Ambrose decided to throw off the monastic garb and life in favour of taking up farming and making Gladys his wife. They made plans to this end, and in order to allow Ambrose to get away it was arranged that Gladys should get him a suitable disguise and meet him at a particular spot not far from the Strid. Gladys seemingly had to cross the river at a certain ford to meet her lover, but according to the story she must have chosen the leap at the Strid as the nearest. She fell in and this time Ambrose failed to save her. He was near at hand and without a thought of the danger of the rocky channel he dived in. His head struck a stone and he was stunned. The rapids of the Strid claimed two more victims.

Apparently some foresters, who were wood-cutting at the time witnessed the tragedy from a distance, and next day both bodies were recovered. The brethren at the Priory had no knowledge of Ambrose's intentions, for a solemn Requiem was offered for the repose of his soul, and his noble effort to save the life of Gladys was entered in the Canonical Book of Beatification. Fanciful visitors to the Strid had declared that the cries of Gladys are sometimes still to be heard. Some have gone further. The figures of the monk and the girl, they declared, occasionally appear transformed and transfigured into the ethereal loveliness of spirits and angels.

Such are the legends and tales of the Strid. The rocky channel narrows the Wharfe from fifty feet to four feet and the results can be imagined. There have been many fatal accidents at this spot and it is not improbable that further tragedies will occur with people who are not content merely to regard the Strid in awe. But in any case—

> *This striding-place is called the Strid,*
> *A name which it took of yore;*
> *A thousand years hath it borne that name,*
> *And shall a thousand more.*

Fred Metcalfe (1954)

THE DEVIL'S BRIDGES

WESTMORLAND has made much of its Devil's Bridge, at Kirkby Lonsdale, and it is rather regrettable that the Yorkshire Dale country does not make more capital out of its own bridge with a similar story. The customary legend, of course, is that the Evil One built bridges in return for favours.

The tale has long been attached to the bridge that spans the turbulent River Dibb, where it crosses the Grassington-Pateley Bridge road after rushing madly down from the heights of Grimwith to join the Wharfe. Yorkshire's variation of the legend avers that Dibble Bridge was built by Satan to facilitate the journeys of a cobbler, who travelled from Thorpe to Fountains Abbey with sandals for the months.

The Yorkshire version, indeed, goes one better than the tales told of the other Devil's Bridges, for it relates how the Thorpe shoemaker was wily enough to flatter His Satanic Majesty, and so (with true Yorkshire artfulness) got the bridge built without forfeiting his soul or anything else.

Actually, the Dales have another bridge reputed to be of Satanic origin, and though the story of its erection is almost exactly like that told about the much better known Westmorland example, here again a cunning Yorkshireman outwitted the Devil. This second Devil's Bridge is officially known as Kilgram Bridge, and it stands not far from Jervaulx Abbey, Wensleydale. It is said that Satan was tricked by the removal of one stone from the structure. The bridge was therefore unfinished – and how could the Evil One claim his forfeit for something that was uncompleted?

Whether the present Kilgram Bridge lacks a stone is uncertain, for it is not the original bridge. The earliest one at this point was built at the beginning of the 16th century, and it has been repaired or entirely rebuilt several times. But the existing structure is sufficiently old to attract the attention of the antiquarian. It is also noteworthy from the scenic point of view. Look upstream from the parapet and you are gazing upon the beauties of Wensleydale.

Arthur Gaunt (1961)

A WHARFEDALE legend was told to me by an old Dalesman, Robert Kidd, of Hartlington. It must be nearly half a century that we were walking up Hebden Bank and as we were passing by Dibbles Bridge he pointed to a group of rocks on the skyline looking over towards Pateley Bridge. He told me that the rocks were known as the "Devil's Apron", and gave me the following legend:

"The Devil was returning to Gerston (Grassington) from Pateley one stormy winter's night and when he got to the Dib, the stream that runs from Grimwith into the Wharfe at Hartlington, he found that a great flood had washed the bridge away, and he was unable to get across. Nothing daunted he went back to Brimham Rocks and filled his apron with stone to build a bridge. He then took a bee line across country back to the Dib, but just as he was crossing the hill his apron strings broke and deposited the stones, apron and all, where they remain to this day. That is why they are named the Devil's Apron. How or when the devil got back to Grassington he did not say."

J. S. Fielden (1943)

LEGENDS OF BRIMHAM ROCKS

A GUIDE book to Brimham Rocks, printed about thirty years ago, narrates a legend connected with the crag known as the Lovers' Leap. A young couple, Julia and Edwin, had eloped and were fleeing across the moors, pursued by Julia's father. Preferring to die rather than be parted, they jumped together from the top of one of the rocks, but a good fairy caused them to reach the earth unharmed. Julia's father was so impressed by this miracle, that he consented to their marriage, and the rock from which they jumped is still called the Lovers' Leap.

This is an old superstition connected with the Wishing Rock. Apparently you will have good luck if you put the middle finger of your right hand into a little hole in the rock and silently wish. One lady in bygone days is said to have travelled from the South of England just to wish in this way.

Another old saying declares that the unsteady Boat Rocking Stone will only move if touched by an honest man. It is also said that Mother Shipton once hid three outlaws in the Druid's Caves.

Ian Dewhirst (1959)

SAWLEY'S GIBBET STONE

A QUARTER of a mile up a green lane, off the Sawley-Bishop Thornton Road and near a stone wall surrounding a large field, stands Sawley's gibbet stone. The stone is a mystery, no records having any allusion to it. The stone is no "thing of beauty" – just a plain stone on a square base, weathered by the wind, rain and snow, and used as a perching post by the birds.

Facing south-east, to the right is Hebden Wood, and hereby hangs a gruesome tale associated with the stone.

A young man and woman held a tryst in the then dark and sinister Hebden Wood. A quarrel ensued and screams were heard, of which no notice was taken. Soon afterward the wood yielded up its grim secret. The woman had been murdered and buried together with her unborn twins.

Many years passed. In a far country, some say America, a man walked into a tavern and ordered a drink, and called this strange toast: "To the ewe and two lambs buried in Hebden Wood." Strangely enough, two men present had heard of the murder. An arrest was made and a trial followed. The murderer was chained to this stone which overlooks the scene of his crime. Some say he lived for seven years, which is beyond all reason; others say a few months, before he died a raving maniac.

To this day there is a lane called "Careless Lane", and a house called "Careless House". It is said the people living in this house heard the shrieks of the hapless woman and let them pass unheeded. This is hardly likely, however, as the house is too far away.

Another story of the stone is that it was once a plague stone. I have also heard that it marks the scene of a battle in the Wars of the Roses. Be that as it may, there it stands as baffling as the Sphinx of Egypt.

M. B. Jolly (1957)

SYLVAN SEMERWATER

A PAINTING depicting the beauties of Semerwater, set me thinking nostalgically of the lake in its sylvan setting. Situated one and a half miles south-west of Bainbridge, and with the limestone ridge of Addleborough rearing itself to the east, its surroundings are reminiscent of the Lake District, which is not far distant, after all.

At one time known as Simmerwater, the tale is often associated with a legend which has been handed down to posterity. No one seems to be aware of its origin, but ut has been coupled with a landslide or minor earthquake, which brought disaster to Raydale and the inhabitants thereabout.

The story unfolds itself with the advent of the Christian era, when a thriving township, astride a rippling stream, was thought to stand on the site of the present lake. Through its streets, in the depth of winter, wandered an angel in the guise of a time-worn old man, scantily clothed, famished with hunger and with no money to buy food and raiment. He sought sustenance and shelter for the night, but nobody would take him in.

Eventually, he arrived at the eastern end of the dale, where he sighted a primitive hutment, wherein lived a kind, elderly couple, who supplied his wants. Beneath their humble roof he was made welcome, given eatables and a night's repose.

Up betimes the next morning, he blessed his benefactors, yet was bitterly disposed towards the awakening community, who had so despised him. In a consuming rage and spreading out his hands in the direction of their dwellings, he pronounced a malediction in terms of "Semerwater rise, Semerwater sink," etc.

To the accompaniment of a terrific hissing sound, the earth was rent asunder, and the meandering stream became a lake, whose swirling waters engulfed the valley. So widespread is the legend, it is said, that even today some dale dwellers, with vivid imaginations, apparently, tell us that the roofs of houses can sometimes be seen beneath the silent waters.

E. Radcliffe (1960)

THE LEGEND
OF SEMERWATER

So fair the city smiled before his gaze.
The ragged stranger rose, his weary limbs
New charged with life, his tired, sunken eyes
Aglow with thoughts of rest, of food and drink.
How brave the towers glowed, and minarets
In shining splendour smote the sunlit sky.
With fresh endeavour up the grievous hill.
The beggar toiled, and reached the shining gate.
Ah, spent was he, in sore and needy plight,
But full of thankfulness his trusting heart,
For here, amidst such plenty he would find
Some kindly hearts to ease his dire distress.
Alas, he looked in vain for friendly face.
His rags inspired rough jeers as through the streets
He made his lone way. The passers by
Were hard with love of gold; no pity shone
Within their worldly eyes. No hand outstretched
To succour him who toiled so slowly on.

The darkness fell, and with it crept that chill
Which is of night, when chairs are drawn around
The homely hearth. When lighted windows smile,
In warm contentment with the scene within.
The ragged stranger knew not where to go.
And then, from out a dwelling, small and old,
A kindly soul came forth, and took him in.
"Thy face is pale with weariness. Rest here."
The gentle voice, compassionate and low,
Was like sweet balm upon the tired heart.
And grateful was he for the simple meal
So swiftly set before him. "Friend," he said,
"In all this wealthy city thou alone
"Art rich; for in thy heart is sympathy,
"Kind pity and compassion, priceless things,
"In this harsh world, where avarice and greed
"Hold such large sway."

The morning came, and up the beggar rose.
And seeing him, his host grew faint with fear.
This countenance was of no earthly man.
The grievious rags had turned to shining robes.
It was an angel who had shared his roof.
And turning to him then, the angel spoke,
"Be not afraid, for blessed thou shalt be.
"But this fair city with its evil heart,
"Is doomed." He cried in wrath, and lo,
A wild wind blew with shrieking voice that seemed
As though a thousand demons were let loose
From Hell.
Then came great floods; swift, savage, piled on high,
With roar terrific. And that city fair
Was swamped and drowned, except that one poor house,
Wherein had lodged the angel in disguise.
And now above that city dreams a lake.
And even yet, 'tis said on summer nights,
The glistening minarets, the houses fair,
Can still be seen beneath the waters bright.
Madge Ellis (1961)

TALES FROM RICHMOND

A CLASSIC legend links Swaledale with King Arthur and his Knights of the Round Table and declares that the King and his followers still sleep there in an underground vault awaiting the hour when England needs their services again.

Everyone in Richmond knows the story of Potter Thompson, but for others who do not here it is: The potter had gone to the river bank to escape his wife's nagging tongue. He spied an opening in the rock beneath the castle, and with the idea of escape still strong in his mind, soon found himself in a subterranean passage, and finally in a huge cavern. Around the walls hung shields and arms. On the floor lay a number of armoured knights, and in the centre, on a raised dais, lay a regal bearded figure grasping a huge sword. Thompson, with Yorkshire curiosity, touched the monster sword. Instantly all the sleepers stirred. So he, with Yorkshire caution, withdrew his hand, The sleepers became immovable once more. Thompson decided to go and tell his wife about it. He found his way outside again. He told his wife, and he told a man who recognised, from his description of the shields, the arms of Arthur and the Knights of the Round Table. Unfortunately the entrance to the cave could not be found again, so Potter Thompson had the honour of being the only man who ever entered the legendary dormitory of the great British king and his knights.

He might have had a greater honour if he had not fled so hastily, for it is recorded that as he fled a deep voice boomed behind him, saying:–

Potter, Potter Thompson!
If thou had'st either drawn
The sword or blown the horn,
Thou'dst been the luckiest man
That ever yet was born.

The poor fellow, of course, could never find the place again. And since then even ubiquitous servants of the Office of Works have failed to find King Arthur's apartment.

Another take from Richmond concerns the legendary treasure of the Castle. Centuries ago some soldiers quartered in the castle resolved to test the truth of an old take that an underground passage ran from the castle to Easby Abbey. But they didn't like the thought of making the journey through such a long, dark tunnel with its precarious roof and foul air, so they got hold of a little drummer boy, filled his head with the tales of the treasure and sent him off alone.

Away he went through the dark passage, playing boldly on his drum; while the soldiers, listening to its muffled rolling, followed above ground through the streets of the town. The sound of the drum became fainter and fainter until, when they reached the spot now occupied by Richmond Grammar School, it ceased altogether.

And that was the last that anyone ever saw of the little drummer boy, so no one knows whether he found the treasure. But on a quiet night you can still hear, very faint and distant, the long rolling of a drum underground. Or so they say.

(1943)

J.J.THOMLINSON

RICHMOND'S LITTLE DRUMMER BOY

They say it is true; the story is old,
Of the underground way, and the dummer boy bold.
It happened in Richmond a long time ago,
When soldiers were stationed there: Oh, what a show
They made in their uniforms, gallant and brave,
With proud colours flying, and bright plumes a-wave.
They marched and they drilled; they swore and they sang,
They ogled the maids till the curfew rang.
And so it is told, that during their stay,
They heard of a secret and underground way.
And it was important, the officers knew,
That someone should try and find a way through.

They chose the small drummer boy. Eager was he
To do and to dare, and right cheerfully,
He entered the cavern which looked black as night,
And, smartly saluting, he marched out of sight.
With a rat-a-tat tat, he beat a tatoo,
So the men above could follow him through
The maze of dark tunnels, as onward he went,
The brave little drummer boy, stern and intent.
With a rat-a-tat atat, and a rat-a-tat tat,
To the castle it led them, and then, after that,
To the old market square, and onwards, away.
They followed excited, so where Easby lay,
A little old village beyond Richmond town,
And still on they went, while a cold sky looked down.

Then all of a sudden, as though a bolt dropped,
They were hushed into silence; the drumming had stopped.
They stood and they stared; they waited; they strained
To catch any sound, but the silence remained.
Oh, what was the reason? Oh, what had occurred?
For though they still listened, no drummer was heard.
No rat-a-tat tat; no rhythmical sound
Came cheerfully up from that dark underground.

And never again was the drummer boy seen.
Though the soldiers all waited, and listened between
Their marching and drilling, for long after that.
But never again did they hear the rat tat
Of the little boy's drum. He had vanished away,
But yet, it is whispered, that even today,
If anyone listens intently and still,
Above that dark spot, he most certainly will
Hear distant and faint, but clear for all that,
The sound of a drum beating rat-a-tat tat.

Madge Ellis (1956)

CLINSCHOR'S KINGDOM

WHERE is Li gweiz prelljus? A knowledge of Medieval French will not help much to find the Ford Perilous. What is needed is an encyclopaedic familiarity with the King Arthur stories, with the ancient tracks and rocks of Britain and, perhaps, with the geology and topography of the Yorkshire Dales, especially the Ingleborough area.

The hunt began with an innocent-looking inquiry from Sam Brewster, of Tadcaster, the defender of bridleways for knights errant. He wrote to ask whether I thought that the words "becca" and "pecca" could be connected with the Saxon "wicca" for "wizard". It did not seem a very likely connection, but I asked why. Mr. Brewster has replied with letters so fascinating that I have kept dashing around the dales following up what appeared to be clues. Sometimes they appeared so to him, sometimes to me. All the same, I have felt a bit like Sir Gawain himself.

For it is Sir Gawain, that redoubtable champion of Arthur's Round Table, who leaped Li gweiz prelljus in the Land of Wonders, on the road that leads to the enchanter Clinschor's Castle of Wonders. Mr. Brewster, who knows his Arthurian homework, thought it possible that the castle was the fort on the summit of Ingleborough. That was why he wondered whether Pecca might indicate the Wizard Falls and give a clue to the Ford Perilous. But although it called it "the longest of long shots," he was not really a shot in the dark.

"Li gweiz prelljus" is the name given to the great leaping-point in the "Parzival" legend recounted in the 12th century by the German poet Wolfram von Eschenbach. "He heard the roar of a waterfall; it had worn away a ravine wide and deep and impassable," says the translation of Von Eschenbach by Helen M. Mustard and Charles E. Passage. "The valiant Gawain dug in his spurs and urged the horse on to the leap." The incident was also recounted about the same time by the French writer Chretien de Troyes. But Cretien spoke of the fords "de Galvoie", which has been taken to mean "of Galloway".

This might be thought to kill the Ingleborough idea stone dead, but

for the very ancient track called "Galloway Gale" which goes from Dent northwards over the hills into Mallerstang, and down the Eden valley into Westmorland and on to Scotland. Southwards from Dent it is traced by Deepdale and down Kingsdale. From there the track is believed to have gone along the Twistleton Lane "green road" across the river Doe at the head of Pecca Falls, over the "back road" between Ingleton and Chapel-le-Dale, across the Moor and away to London – with perhaps an older route to Somerset.

Pecca Falls are a charming place to visit even without an excuse. The search for a possible "gweiz" made it still more pleasant. From Ingleton the path ascends beside the Doe through gorges of impressive height and gloom, and alongside thundering waterfalls, one on top of another. They are beautiful to look at. But above the sheer sides of the ravine are deep banks which slope so steeply that it is impossible to imagine even a fabulous horse leaping across. Only above Thornton Force was there a possible place – and here a horse could get across easily enough without leaping at all. The report to Mr. Brewster had to be a reluctant negative.

In the course of this search, however, the Galloway Gate kept on coming into discussion; and then I was told of a place actually on that old road where people traditionally leapt across a chasm. But it was far beyond Dent – in fact, it was at Hell Gill, where the infant river Eden forms the border between Yorkshire and Westmorland in Mallerstang.

The road runs just above Hell Gill Farm. This is the track along which the formidable Anne Clifford, Countess of Pembroke, travelled in her coach from Skipton Castle to Pendragon and on to Brougham. But how did she get her coach across Hell Gill? At that point the ravine is not much more than a yard or so wide – but it is 100 feet deep! She must have had her retinue make a temporary wooden bridge. Nowadays there is a substantial arch, but to look over the parapet down into the gloomy gulf is a startling experience.

If Hell Gill were the "gweiz prelljus", the only site for the Castle of Wonders would be Pendragon – which is about six miles away. It did not seem to be sufficiently impressive. Moreover, as Mr. Brewster pointed out, there is always a feeling in the old poem of looking up to the Castle – whereas Pendragon is lower than Hell Gill. The Gill can also be jumped on foot if one has the nerve. Again, the hunt seemed to have drawn a blank. Returning from Hell Gill through Ribblehead towards Ingleton, I was seized once again by the sight of Ingleborough looming majestically overhead. Why, of course, the old road crossed first the Doe and then – nearer Ingleborough – the Twiss. How could one have forgotten that? The two valleys run into one, and are known collectively as "Ingleton waterfalls". This time I went up the eastern branch, through Twistleton Glen.

One after another, from the first dramatic footbridge upwards, were places where it was just possible to think of a fabulous knight on a fabulous horse making a huge leap across the chasm, and being able to climb up the far side afterwards. The river itself was much more impressive – more worth-while leaping over. Well up the glen, the path climbs a concrete but discrete staircase beside a gorge of unsurpassed beauty. A roaring cascade comes down in tumbling white foam beside the track. At the top of the staircase, the path edges round a crag, and emerges high above a great bowl. I looked across and down to a narrow rift where the river forced a way between two great rocks. Below that was a whirlpool and a shelving beach. From there the stream vanishing into the roaring cascade.

What was it Sam Brewster had written? "It would be necessary to find a place near a high waterfall where the tops of the ravine on each side are level enough and not too far apart."

In addition – since Gawain and his great horse fell into the water at the first attempt – the leap could not itself be across a deep chasm. The horse was swept by the whirlpool to a sloping bank where the knight was able to pull it out. This spot seemed to fit every requirement. Just below there was even a great yew tree spanning the ravine – just such a tree as the one from which Gawain had to break a bough for a wreath for the duchess whom he was escorting on his adventure.

If this is in fact "Li gweiz prelljus", then Ingleborough is the Magician Clinschor's castle where he kept many women imprisoned, and the whole area around is the "Land of Wonders". And once the map is drawn up from that point of view, it is remarkable how well the jigsaw of clues seems to fall into shape.

"Caution!" I think I hear Mr. Brewster cry. He himself writes: "When one has a theory, all sorts of things stimulate thought – the name Kingsdale, for example." All right, but for me the top of Twistleton Glen will always be the Perilous Leap.

G. Ragland Phillips (1973)

Part 2

Yorkshire Hauntings

GHOST STORIES WERE TOLD BY FIRELIGHT

WE hear a lot about the power of the spoken word. Powerful it has certainly become when one man in a small room can speak to millions through the medium of wireless. Yet I think that even more powerful than the voice of the broadcaster was the voice of the Dales story-teller on winter's nights long ago.

His audience rarely exceeded a dozen and was made up of relatives and friends, but his voice had the power to excite and interest, depress and uplift, stimulate and exalt. His allies were the firelight and the whining wind, and it was uncanny the way the very young and the very old responded alike to his message.

The wireless does most of the entertaining on Christmas Eve in these days, but I like to look back upon the times when Christmas Eve for me meant the visit of an uncle with a fund of stories. When supper was over he fell naturally into his stride. The oil lamps were extinguished and we settled back in our chairs to listen. The firelight danced across the walls and ceiling of the room, and uncle's rich voice competed with the homely crackle of the logs.

I do not recall he ever told a story twice, though he visited us on

Christmas Eve for many years, and he never went far afield for his material. It was not so much what he said but the way he said it. He created an atmosphere in which he could play with our emotions, and he could change the pattern of the tale by the inflection of his voice. His favourite stories were ghost stories.

Yorkshire has a wonderful range and variety of ghost stories, and from the mouth of a good story teller they are still capable of raising shivers on Christmas Eve, as they did in times gone by. I remember uncle telling us of that famous spectre of the western dales – the barguest; of the creature "big as a little-ish bear, and yellow, with great eyes like saucers," to quote a man who years ago declared he saw it. The barguest haunted Upper Wharfedale, particularly the wild region about Troller's Ghyll, and dalesfolk would declare that those who caught its eye were sure to die. Here, then, is a simple test by which anyone can identify a barguest!

One of my favourite ghost stories is that which links itself with Beggar's Wife Bridge, between Settle and Giggleswick. In the name of the bridge is a hint of the story. A beggar took a sudden dislike to his wife and promptly killed her at the bridge. The poor woman's ghost has since been reported as "rushing about with nothing but a cob-web for her face". It is stated the ghost looks fearfully behind, which suggests that the beggar's wife is herself haunted by the ghost of her husband.

Kirkby Overblow has its phantom hound, and legend declares that a farmer in the district forgot his dog, which he had left guarding some sheep, and went home to bed. The sheepdog whined and scratched at the farmhouse door in the early hours of the morning, but no one let it in, so it wandered away to starve. Today its ghost is said to haunt the local fields looking for the master who forgot. This story seems very improbable. Which Dales farmer would forget his dog? And which Dales sheepdog, once forgotten, would leave its post to return whining home without permission?

Edward Garratt, one-time schoolmaster of Romaldkirk, used to tell of the first time he saw a ghost: "I was staying with my father on his farm in Teesdale and was going to the local inn to fetch some tobacco when something arose in front of me. It was a little boy wearing a fustian coat, with a red, round cap on his head. He looked at me and smiled, and then vanished into the hedge.

"I told this to one of the servants. 'Oh,' he said, not at all surprised, 'that will be little Jack Stevens. He was missed when folks were loading coals into a truck out Cockfield way, and he wasn't seen any more until they found him dead in the bottom of the truck when they took the coals out again. He'd be walking along the roads he loved'."

Most of the Yorkshire ghost stories have a practical explanation, but there are tales of supernatural phenomena which offer no explanation. The Rev. James Macnabb, one-time Rector of Bolton Abbey, said that in 1911 he was standing by the window of an empty bedroom in the Rectory when he turned round and saw an apparition standing in a doorway. Immediately he moved, the figure – that of a monk – disappeared. The same thing happened on another occasion.

There was no authentic explanation for the appearance of the ghost, but it has been suggested the figure was that of a monk who has been murdered for the sake of relics he had been carrying from one community to another, and that the body was thrown into a space in the walls of the Rectory.

An unusual story of ghostly associations came from York. Clementhorpe is not a populous area of the old city, but before building commenced the district was pasture land and here the Archbishop Scrope was beheaded in 1405 at the insistance of Henry IV after a travesty of a trial at Bishopthorpe. In the field at Clementhorpe the prelate was first buried, but later the body was removed to the Minster.

Until just over a century ago belated travellers in the locality reported seeing a coffin suspended in the air and slowly floating along. It was covered with a black pall fringed with white silk, and behind it walked the Archbishop in his robes, an open book in his hand from which he read rapidly, though no sound issued from the moving lips. The phantom disappeared as suddenly as it had appeared.

Why the Archbishop should conduct his own funeral service and how his head was restored to his shoulders no one has been able to explain. Explanation is not likely to be forthcoming, for it is impossible today to identify the exact site where the Archbishop was executed.

One of Yorkshire's popular stories is that of the ghostly lady who haunted the road between Pickering and York. She had been the betrothed of a coach driver, of Sheriff Hutton, but on the day fixed for her wedding she had jilted her lover and eloped with a young gallant who won her with fine promises and brave talk.

Alas he betrayed her and later divulged that he was already married. She fled from him with her baby and waited by the roadside for her former lover's coach. To him she confessed and begged forgiveness, and in return for his promise to look after her child, promised, in her dying breath, to come back in spirit form and protect him and his descendants from the dangers of the road.

Many years later, when the grandson of her first love was driving one moonlight night from Malton to York, a spectral figure of a woman stepped into the road and signalled the driver to stop. To the wonderment of the passengers of the coach, he did and turned back to Malton, pleading as an excuse a broken spring of his coach. Later that night three masked men were apprehended at Barton corner where they lay in wait for the coach. The dying promise of the betrayed girl had been fulfilled to the grandson of her lover.

Mary Queen of Scots is said to haunt the old Wensleydale mansion, Nappa Hall, where that tragic queen once spent two nights as guest of the famous Sir Christopher Metcalfe. A visitor to the Hall claimed to see the apparition in 1878, when it entered the hall and walked away in the direction of the dais.

"Thinking it was the farmer's wife," the visitor afterwards said, "I ran after her and was going to touch her when she turned round and I saw her face. It was very lovely. Her dress seemed to be made of black velvet. After looking at me for a moment, she went on and disappeared through the door leading to the winding stone staircase in the angle turret of the West tower. Her face, figure and general appearance reminded me of portraits of Mary Queen of Scots."

Such were the tales told round the fireside on Christmas nights by our grandparents and their predecessors, and no "thrillers" of today stirred the blood and made the heart beat faster than these stories founded on facts and tradition and handed on as legends from one generation to another.

Yorkshire has countless stores of such stories. Every great house and every old abbey have their spectres; bridges and cross-roads, meres and commons, each had their "boggard" or spirit. Woe betide those who laughed at these people of a ghostly world, for ghosts have ears and an unerring way of vengeance.

'S'sh, what was that?

Frank Harrison (1951)

PHANTOM OF THE WOLDS

I WAS once commissioned to write six ghost stories for a local paper. The stories would run concurrently for the six weeks before Christmas, and they had to be original! Which, as you can imagine, set me quite a task, for there are believers and unbelievers where ghosts are concerned. I quickly realised that the believers "run in a family", which made me realise, too, how ideas and superstitions are handed down from parents to children.

I do not scoff at the supernatural. I do not understand it, anymore than I understand wireless or television. Some folk are psychic, and it was these folk I searched out, with some success. As it's Christmas once again, I'll tell you about a visit to an old farmhouse.

There was a bitter wind blowing and the frozen snow lay deep in the stubble field I had to cross, but I had talked with a relative of the people who were occupying the little farmhouse. I was told that when a child was staying for a holiday, she had come downstairs and asked who was the nice lady in one of the bedrooms.

As nobody in the household happened to be upstairs at the time, this caused some uneasiness. It was known that the place, which is near the coast, had once been the haunt of smugglers. In fact, it was said that the property had changed hands with money purchased from stolen bonds. When, after the war, another wing was built on to the old place, the new accommodation was used for sleeping quarters.

The old house, so the family said, was haunted and nobody used the upstairs rooms. One of the sons, however, had made a friend while he was in the Forces; this friend called, and as the weather was inclement he hinted that he would like to stay the night. His friend was keen for him to do so, but when the idea was put to his mother she shied away from it, knowing that all the bedrooms were occupied except those in the old house.

Her son was not to be put off. A bed must be aired for his friend. Blankets were taken to a small room under the eaves, and the evening was spent in yarning and smoking. Ultimately the family retired. The visitor owned up the next day that he had had a strange feeling of loneliness and apprehension the minute he was left to ascend the stairs to his room. Undressed, and into bed, he didn't want to put out the light, and when he did so at once regretted it and wished he had left the candle burning.

So, worrying and fretting, he at last dozed off, only to wake after a brief sleep with the knowledge that someone was standing by the bed looking at him. He lay quite still, bathed in perspiration, knowing that the candle was close to hand yet afraid to reach for it. Nothing stirred but there seemed to be a quiet rustle in a far corner where a curtain had been hung. Could somebody be hiding behind that curtain?

He slept fitfully, waking periodically to feel that other presence in the room, and not daring to stir until with daylight, his friend came. Told of the other's feelings, the son of the house did not scoff. "The family thought I was spinning them a yarn," he said, "when I came home and slept here. Your experiences have proved me right. I would sooner sleep on the kitchen hearthrug than spend another night up here."

Yet neither of the lads had seen anything. A presence had threatened them – a ghost of some past miscreant, perhaps a smuggler. The yarn that treasure was buried near the old farmhouse may be correct. A Preventive Officer is said to have died there one stormy night.

The place is very old, and so are the stories told about it.

Florence Hopper (1976)

THE SCREAMING SKULL OF BURTON AGNES

YORKSHIRE is rich in ghost stories – churchyard hauntings, phantom funerals, headless spectres, the midnight coach, ghosts of the famous and the unknown. They range the county from the isolated hamlets to the large towns and are both old and new. In bygone times ghosts were often the main topic during winter nights round the fireside. Stories about them were told and retold in cosy inn parlours and recorded by village parsons and students of local lore. They are of all time and many places.

Some of these stories were told to me by my uncle when I was a boy at Thirsk. He lived in the town for nearly all his long life and, like his father before him, he was a keen student of the lore of the district. For other Yorkshire hauntings I have referred to Christina Hole's *Haunted England*, William Henderson's *Folk Lore of the Northern Counties*, and Elliott O'Donnell's *Haunted Churches*.

One of the most celebrated of all ghost stories is that of the screaming skull of Burton Agnes Hall, near Driffield, a haunting which has its origin in a girl's passionate love for the home she had helped to build.

The estate originally belonged to the De Somervilles and in the reign of Edward I, it passed to the Griffiths family. Sir Henry Griffiths died in the early 17th century, leaving his three daughters as co-heiresses. They decided to create a new and more convenient home, and the oldest part of the present lovely mansion was built for them.

Anne Griffiths, the youngest girl, watched it grow in beauty and state-liness with intense affection. It was ready in 1628 but Anne was not destined to enjoy it for long. Soon after the three sisters moved in, Anne paid a visit to the St. Quintins at Harpham Hall about a mile away, feeling perfectly safe in the protection of her favourite dog, even though at that time the roads were infested with beggars and ruffians. It was a moonless night, and she had reached St. John's Well when she heard the tramp of heavy footsteps behind her. Turning round, she saw two men coming towards her.

"Alms, my lady," a gruff voice demanded, and as she was opening her wallet, the men noticed that she was wearing a valuable ring. "Thy ring, my lady, will serve us better than alms," he declared.

Anne protested spiritedly and the men struck her across the head with cudgels, took the ring off her finger and made off leaving her unconscious in the roadway. He was found and carried to Harpham Hall, and the next day she was brought back to Burton Agnes Hall, where she died five days later.

Shortly before she died, Anne regained consciousness and made her sisters promise that her head should be kept in the house she so much loved. She threatened to make it uninhabitable if the promise was not kept. Her sisters, probably thinking that this strange request was the outcome of delirium, made no attempt to comply with it, and she was buried in the ordinary way in the family vault.

A few days after the funeral, a loud crash was heard in an upper room, and although an immediate search was made nothing was found to account for it. Two or three nights later, the whole household was roused by the violent slamming of doors, groans and other extraordinary noises, and these continued for several days.

The two Miss Griffiths remembered their broken promise and decided to consult the Vicar as to what they should do. He advised them to open Anne's grave and bring her head back to the house. When this was done, the noises ceased. Local tradition had it that although the body was found to be perfect, the head had somehow become detached from it and was already a skull.

So long as it remained in the house, nothing unusual happened, but when, some years later, an attempt was made to bury it in the garden, the consequent noises were so horrifying that it had to be dug up again. On one occasion a servant who was unaware of the story threw it out of the window on to a passing hay cart, with the result that both horses and cart became immovably fixed and unable to stir until the terrified girl confessed what she had done and the skull was returned to its place. Footsteps and the rustling of a silk dress were occasionally heard, and these the servants christened "Awd Nance".

It seems that Anne's spirit still haunts her old house, for there is a tradition of a fawn lady who is occasionally seen. In Lord Halifax's *Ghost Book* a letter from Mrs. Wickham Boynton is quoted in which she tells him of two ghostly experiences at the Hall.

One day in 1915, Mrs. Wickham Boynton was seated in the Hall when she saw a thin small woman in a fawn dress come through the garden and go up the steps to the front door. Thinking she was a visitor, she asked her husband to go and bring her in. He went, but returned immediately saying that there was no-one there.

Mrs. Wickham Boynton then remembered the traditional ghost of Anne Griffiths, whose sister had married Sir Matthew Boynton and so brought the estate into the possession of the Boyntons. Some years before, Mrs. Wickham Boynton had seen this fawn lady hurrying up steps in the same manner on the east front of the house.

Shortly before Anne Griffiths' skull was bricked up in the walls of the Hall, John Bilton, whose relative, Matthew Potter, was a gamekeeper at the Hall, came to Burton Agnes to spend his Christmas holidays and Potter invited him to sleep at the Hall for a night or two.

"The Hall's badly haunted," Potter informed Bilton, "And if thou's afraid of ghosts, thee'd better sleep somewhere else."

Bilton, apparently untouched by any sort of superstition, replied, "Nay, I don't care how many spirits you've got so long as they're in bottles!

Potter then told his young relative the story of "Awd Nance", and asked if he would like to see her portrait. So they went to the room where the portrait of Anne Griffiths, by Marc Geerarts, was hanging. Then, as John Bilton lifted his candle closer to the portrait to have a

better look at it, a gust a air extinguished the flame, and even when he had relit the candle the same thing happened, so that they were obliged to grope their way to the bedroom in the dark.

For a while Bilton lay awake pondering over the strange tale of the haunted skull, and the mysterious gusts of air which had extinguished his candle. The bright, frosty, full moon was gleaming through the mullion windows, and behind the funereal, plush curtains he imagined he saw something luminous which roughly resembled the shape of a woman in a curious lace robe.

He was about to awake his gamekeeper relative who was sleeping soundly in the bed next to his, when he realised that the apparition was nothing more than a rabbit net draped over Potter's coat and hat hanging between the curtains. "Nerves, that what it is," he muttered. "High time I was asleep any way."

No sooner had he recovered from the shock than he heard the sound of shuffling feet outside the bedroom door. Then after a long pause, the bedroom door was flung open, and footsteps entered the room and moved towards the window. His heart pounding wildly, Bilton jumped out of bed and seized Potter's arm. "Matty," he gasped. "Room's haunted – noises and footsteps –"

Potter yawned indifferently. "Haunted?" he repeated, and added: "Jinny Yewlets, I suppose. Them owls come inside on cold nights to roost on the kingposts and what with their hooting and scrimmaging they make a devil of a noise –"

Bilton gazed round the faintly moonlit room, now strangely quiet. "It was no owls, Matty," he replied solemnly, "Nay it was like some body –"

Potter yawned wearily and turned over to go to sleep. "Then it must be Awd Nance," he mumbled.

"Awd Nance," Bilton repeated uneasily. "Sounded more like Old Nick to me!"

For a while Bilton sat thoughtfully on the edge of the gamekeeper's bed, then with a weary sigh he shuffled across to his own bed and snuggled deeply under the bedclothes. The full moon shining brightly through the window seemed to intensify the eerie silence, and for a while he lay awake listening for the slightest sound.

At last he seemed to doze off into a restless sleep, but suddenly awoke with a pounding heart. The shuffling footsteps had returned to the door and as he peered over the bedclothes, he saw the door slowly open and the figure of a woman shrouded in a misty, purplish light stood in the doorway. For a moment or two the apparition stood still and silent, then suddenly vanished towards the window. All was silent again.

"Aye, it was Awd Nance alright," the gamekeeper assured the white-faced young man over breakfast next morning, when Bilton had related his experience. "And judging by the looks of you, it will be a long while before you'll want to spend a night at the Hall again."

William Foggitt (1962)

MOONSHINE

ENTERING the low stone doorway of the old Dales Inn there was no mistaking from the brisk sound of voices in the snug that a forceful argument was in progress. Not that there was anything unusual in this. Only on two occasions do I recall going into the *Pack Horse Inn*, or "t'owd Pack", as it is better known, in silence.

The first time was another wintry Christmas Eve years ago when the Ellington bus skidded on the icy road, carrying all its twenty occupants to eternity in a swift plunge to the river far below. The other was a summer evening in the war days when four bodies lay proud and still on hastily improvised tables, the twisted wreckage of their aircraft silhouetted in the dying light of day high up on Hunter's Fell.

As I made my way into the tiny tap room, bright with its Yuletide decorations, the dispute ceased a moment while half a dozen voices shouted a hasty "Good Evening". Then the wordy battle was resumed.

I beckoned to Fred, the landlord, who, with an understanding nod, retreated and silently returned with a tankard of ale. I took a draught, lit my pipe, and endeavoured to comprehend the cause of the discussion which was fast rising in tempo.

"It's nowt but moonshine," roared Tom Brooke, a powerfully built farmer with a face as red as a chimney pot and certainly as red as the glistening holly berries festooned round the room. As if to give emphasis, he banged on the table with such force that the very glasses rang again.

"That's true, Bill," joined in an extremely tall, thin man, with a three-quarter jacket and a spotted scarf draped with magnificent abandon around his long angular neck. "If Bill says it is so, then I half believe it did happen. I've known Bill nigh on forty years and he doesn't say things for the sake of talking."

"That's a view I would entertain myself," added a dark-coated speaker in a somewhat pompous manner. "As postman one sees a sight of things which never come the way of ordinary farming folk. I remember in '92, or was it '93 ...?"

His recollections were brought to a hasty close by Tom Brooke who, with another mighty blow on the table, rose to his feet and addressed the excited audience. "I say it's moonshine and moonshine it is. A dead man's a dead man, and dead men don't walk about.

"You're like a pack of old women with your tales of dead men walking about as ghosts. T'only ghosts I ever did see were a pair of 'em in Lady Wood, but believe me they were wick enough."

A roar of laughter greeted this sally, which bore reference to an unfortunate and somewhat scandalous incident in which the postman had not been entirely blameless. The tension relaxed and the discomfited guardian of Her Majesty's mail seized the opportunity of masking his indignation by calling to Fred to "bring 'em again."

It was as the landlord was leaving the room to carry out the order that a newcomer entered – an elderly man, but straight upright, with grey hair and a heavy grey moustache. No sooner did Tom Brooke see the stranger than his face broke into a great good-humoured smile of recognition.

"By the Lord Harry, if it isn't Sam Barker! By gum! but I'm pleased to see thee. I haven't clapped eyes on thi since last Christmas, but if tha will go and live away fra t'world in that wooden shack on Brigg Moor it is nobbut to be expected. Fred, another pint for Sam."

A general welcome to the stranger seemed to put the recent argument out of mind. While Tom and Sam talked together, the remainder of the company broke into general conversation and – "That's a fine gallower of Jack Thompson's ..." mingled with – "What's this queer story I've been hearing about Seth Webster's lass?" filled the room.

Some while afterwards I glanced at the clock. It was exactly on the stroke of ten. It was some distance to my home and I had a variety of Christmas preparations to carry out, so draining my tankard I rose to leave. So did Sam Barker, who passed out before me.

With a "Good Night and a Merry Christmas" to everyone, I followed Sam to the outer door, with half a mind to ask if he was walking my way.

I increased my step, but strangely enough Sam was not to be seen.

At that moment the moon broke through the racing clouds and all was light, but although I faced up and down, the roadway was completely deserted. I was mystified, but the pressing need for me to be home in good time was uppermost in my thoughts, and so I swing away with long strides to my own fireside.

The following morning I was back at the old *Pack* enjoying a quiet drink before my Christmas evening meal. Fred, the landlord and I were

sitting alone. Suddenly a slow, measured footstep was heard and in came Tom Brooke.

It *was* Tom Brooke, but no longer the Tom Brooke of the previous evening. No longer the Tom Brooke who had shouted and roared away less than twenty-four hours ago. His ruddy face was now sharpened and with a deathly pallor – evidence of intense strain.

Holding out a newspaper, his shaking hands smoothed out a page on the table and an unsteady finger pointed to a paragraph. Fred and I leaned over and I felt my heart beat more quickly as I read aloud a paragraph headed: "Farmer's tragic death".

I went on: "Yesterday afternoon a gamekeeper crossing Brigg Moor came upon the burnt out remains of a wooden building used as a dwelling by Mr. Sam Barker, a retired farmer. Search among the still glowing debris brought to light a charred body which subsequent recognition proved to be that of the unfortunate Mr. Barker. It is not known whether his relatives..."

Here I stopped reading and turning to Fred and Tom muttered: "Poor lonely old devil! To think that only last night he was with us in this very room..." I broke off at the increasing pallor of Tom's face. "That's just it," he breathed, "and I called it moonshine. You see there is no paper published on Christmas Day and this is yesterday morning's paper!"

"Quix" (1965)

THE LADIES
OF WATTON ABBEY

BETWEEN Driffield and Beverley stands a Tudor style of building which goes by the name of Watton Abbey. The original building is supposed to have been a nunnery, founded in the earliest period of Anglo-Saxon Christianity, and destroyed by the Danes in the ninth century. In the twelfth century it is believed to have been refounded by Lord Eustace Fitz-John of Knaresborough, at the instigation of Henry Murdac, Archbishop of York.

Shortly after he became Archbishop in 1147, Murdac placed a little girl of about four years of age at Watton with a view to her ultimately taking the veil. Of this little girl, Mr. F. Ross, who contributed a series of historical and folk-lore sketches to *The Leeds Mercury*, about century ago, wrote:—

"Elfrida was a merry, vivacious little creature and while but a child was a source of amusement to the sisterhood. But as she grew up, her outbursts of merriment and the sallies of wit which began to animate her conversation, were checked as being inconsistent with the character of a young lady who was now enrolled as a novice, preparatory to taking the veil.

"As she advanced towards womanhood Elfrida's form gradually developed into a most symmetrical figure; her features became the perfection of beauty, set off with a transparent delicacy of complexion, such as would have rendered her the centre of attraction even among the beauties of a Royal Court. This aroused the jealousies of the Sisters, who were chiefly middle-aged spinsters and whose homely and somewhat coarse features had proved detrimental to their hopes of obtaining husbands. They began to treat her with scornful looks, chilling neglect and petty persecutions, so that she began to show repugnance to convent life."

Sprightly and light-hearted, Elfrida became desperately unhappy, immured within these unfriendly walls, and she greatly longed to escape and to mingle with the outer world. According to the charter of endowment, the lay brethren of the monastery were entrusted with the management of the secular affairs of the nunnery, which necessitated their admission within its portals on certain occasions for conference with the Prioress. On these occasions, Elfrida would cast furtive and very "un-nun-like" glances at one or two of these young men.

She felt herself drawn to one of them particularly. The young man noticed her furtive glances and was deeply impressed by her beauty.

They found means of having secret meetings at night, when vows of enduring love were exchanged.

Elfrida was summoned to appear before her superiors on a charge of "transgressing the conventional rules and violating one of the most stringent laws of monastic life", and as concealment was impossible, she boldly confessed her fault, adding that she had no vocation for convent life and desired to be banished from the community. This request could not be entertained. The culprit had brought a scandal and indelible strain upon the house, and it must be concealed from the world.

It was variously suggested that she should be burnt to death, walled up alive, and that she should be flayed alive, but the more prudent averted these extreme measures, and suggested some milder form of punishment. Elfrida was stripped, stretched on the floor, and scourged

with rods until the blood tricked down her lacerated back. She was then cast into a foul dungeon, without light, fettered by iron chains to the floor, and supplied with only bread and water, "which was administered with bitter taunts and reproaches."

While lying in the dungeon Elfrida became penitent, and one night, while sleeping in her fetters, Archbishop Murdac appeared to her in a vision and accused her of having cursed him. "I have certainly cursed you for having, in the first place, put me in such an uncongenial sphere," she replied defiantly.

The Archbishop gazed at her solomnly. "Should you not rather curse yourself for yielding to temptation?"

"So I do, your grace," she confessed, "but I regret having imputed the blame on you."

Archbishop Murdac exhorted her to repenitence, and the daily repetition of certain psalms.

The holy sisters were worried as to what should be done with the infant which was expected daily, and preparation was made for its reception. One night, Elfrida was again visited in a vision by the Archbishop. He was accompanied by two women who, "with the aid of the Archbishop, safely delivered her of the infant, which they bore away in their arms, covered by a white cloth".

When the nuns came next morning they found Elfrida in perfect health, and restored to her youthful appearance, without any signs of the accouchement. The next night, all her fetters were miraculously removed, and when the nuns entered her cell the following morning, they found her standing free.

The Father Superior of the convent was called in. He invited Ailred, Abbot of Rievaulx, to investigate the case. Ailred decided that it was a miraculous intervention, and departed saying, "What God hath cleansed, call not uncommon or unclean, and whom He has loosed thou mayst not bind."

What afterwards became of Elfrida is not known, but after these miraculous events it may be presumed that she would be admitted as a member of the sisterhood, despite her little "peccadillo".

There is a haunted room at Watton Abbey, and the spectre which frequents it is popularly known as "The Headless Nun of Watton". Ghost hunters believe, however, that this apparition is not that of the transgressing nun of the twelfth century, but a brutally beheaded lady of the 17th century. Most ghost hunters believe that story-tellers have confused the two traditions, and treated them as one story, regarding the two heroines as identical.

Ailred, Abbot of Rievaulx, vouches for the truth of his narration of Elfrida by saying, "Let no one doubt the truth of this account, for I was an eye-witness to many of the facts, and the remainder were related to me by persons of such mature age and distinguished position that I cannot doubt the accuracy of their statements."

The account of the other unfortunate lady of Watton is much more recent. She was a lady of distinction, a devoted Royalist of the Civil War, and at that time occupied the house at Watton. Her tragic story commences shortly after the memorable Battle of Marston Moor, which was the death blow to the Royalists north of the Humber.

During the late summer of 1644, when the Parliamentarians dominated the broad lands of Yorkshire, a party of fanatical Roundheads came one day to the neighbourhood of Watton "breathing out threatenings and slaughter" against the "malignants". The lady of Watton, who was

a devout Roman Catholic, heard of this band of Puritan soldiers, who were rampaging over the Wolds, and of the barbarous murders of which they were susposed to have been guilty. Her husband was away, fighting in the ranks of the King near Oxford, and she was left without any protector, except a few servants who would be of no use against a band of armed soldiers.

It was with great fear and trembling that she heard that the Puritan soldiers had arrived at Driffield, about four miles away, and when she heard that the marauders were on their march toward Watton, for the purpose of plundering, she shut herself, with her child and her jewels in the wainscotted room, hoping, if necessary, to escape by means of a secret stair.

It was not long before the soldiers arrived, calling loudly for admittance and hammering violently on the door. Failing to meet with any response they went off in search of implements with which to break down the door. Suddenly they noticed a low archway opening on to the moat, which they guessed was a side entrance to the house. Immediately they crossed the moat, and found the stair which they ascended, and came upon the panel, which they concluded was a disguised door. A few heavy blows broke it open, and admitted them into the presence of the lady, who was lying prostrate before a crucifix.

For a few moments the lady lay motionless on the floor, then rising briskly to her feet, she demanded to know what the soldiers wanted and the meaning of their violent intrusion. "We have come to despoil the owner of this mansion," a gruff voice replied. "If he had been present we would have smitten him to death as a worshipper of idols, and an abomination in the sight of God."

The lady gazed defiantly at the rough-faced soldier. "I have heard of your dastardly conduct on the Wolds," she said, "but I cannot believe that you ruffians are a fair specimen of the God-fearing men who fought under Fairfax, and routed Newcastle and Prince Rupert at Marston Moor – the men who fought with the sword in one hand and the Bible in the other."

The soldiers listened impatiently, and gruffly demanded the plate and other valuables of the house. "If you want them you must find them for yourselves, for I have no intention of giving them to you," the lady replied defiantly.

The rough-faced soldier who had spoken to the lady in the first place now glared fiercely into her eyes. "Hew down the woman of Belial with the sword," he ordered his men, and immediately they caught her child from her arms, and dashed its head against the wall. Then they struck down the lady of Watton, and slashed off her head, after which they plundered the house and departed with the spoil.

From that time, it is said, the Ghost of the lady has haunted the room in which this barbarous deed was perpetrated in the summer of 1644. In the present house at Watton, says a ghost hunter, there is a chamber wainscotted throughout with panelled oak, one of the panels forming a door, so accurately fitted that it cannot be distinguished from the other panels. It is opened by a secret spring, and communicates with a stone stair descending to the moat.

It seems probably that the room was a hiding place for the Jesuits or priests of the Roman Catholic Church when they were so ruthlessly hunted down and persecuted in Elizabethan and Jacobean times.

The room is reputed to be haunted by the ghost of a headless lady with an infant in her arms, who comes to sleep there sometimes at night, the bedclothes being found the following morning in a disordered state, as if a person had been sleeping in them. It is said that the ghost appears minus head, attired in blood-stained garments, with her infant in her arms, and stands motionless for a while at the foot of the bed, then vanishes.

Is Watton haunted by the apparitions of both unfortunate women – the twelfth century nun and the seventeenth century Royalist lady?

William Foggitt (1962)

THE "YORK MAIL"

CHRISTMAS Eve, and the first snow of the winter lay thick upon the ground. The sun had set some thirty minutes previously, and the sky was overcast. A bitter cold wind moaned through the trees and blew the white snowflakes in small spirals as the grey light of a winter evening rapidly closed upon the scene.

The "York Mail", a regular coach service between London and York, was already three hours overdue and its weary passengers were beginning to speculate as to whether in fact they would reach their destination before the morning. The guard and driver, wrapped in great coats, mufflers and scarves so that only their eyes peered into the gloom, cursed and lashed the horses as they skidded on the snow-covered road. Five miles from York there is a small valley which was wooded with oaks and sycamores; it was here that the strange events which befell this unfortunate coach occured.

Evening was rapidly turning into night and as the coach passed through the last part of open country the isolated trees, hedgerows and

fences all covered with snow, disappeared into darkness. Situated at the bottom of the small wooded valley and surrounded by tall oaks lay *Ye Olde Oak Inne*, a hospitable and pleasant hostelry for weary travellers.

Feeling the cold and in need of refreshment, the passengers and crew of the coach decided to call at the inn for some ale and food before proceeding to York. Inside the inn, a large blazing log fire greeted the travellers and they were welcomed by the many people celebrating the season. There was ham and bacon to eat with the good Yorkshire ale and so it was not for many hours after, that the travellers decided to continue their journey.

When they came out of the inn it had stopped snowing. The sky was bright and clear and only occasional rifts of clouds covered the full moon, whose white light twinkled in the deep snow.

Among the travellers there was a particularly evil one named George who, upon seeing a poor beggar walk by, began to mock the beggar and throw snow at him. The others, being of similar temperament with the ale, proceeded to do the same until the beggar collapsed dead in the snow. Their hands raw with cold and their throats sore with laughter the travellers returned to the coach and went upon their way laughing heartily.

They had gone but a few yards when a terrible apparition came before them. In the road there appeared six figures, all a ghostly white. They had the bodies of men but faces of wolves and their leader was the devil himself. Such was the sight of these creatures, that all the travellers deserted the coach and fled to the woods. They ran so fast that some believed demons possessed their very bodies. And those who did not collapse exhausted upon the ground in the snow, crushed their skulls against the trunks of trees.

The following morning a search party found the coach with all its mail and valuables intact. But nothing was ever heard again, in this world at least, of the six travellers who fled in madness from the coach, and all that was left to tell the tale were the deep footprints in the snow.

A. Marshall Horner (1968)

A STOOL FOR THE GHOST

IN THE attic at Peartree Farm, "somewhere in the East Riding", there is a stool for a ghost! It is a little wooden stool, a miniature form, cut into "fishtails" at each end: a stool which our grandparents would have called "a cricket".

When the new owners came to Peartree Farm, the children would have dearly loved to bring the little stool downstairs. It was just the thing for children to play with, but their father had heard rumours in the village; he knew of the stool and he knew that to keep the peace in his home the cricket must be left in the attic.

And so it was, but peace did not exactly reign. For one day when one of the teenage daughters went up to her room she saw that though there was no one else in the room with her, the bedclothes were being carefully folded back by an unseen hand. At Christmas time, an unseen hand lifted a decanter while a meal was being cleared away. About the same time a voice called up the stairs during the night and awoke the whole household. A search by the farmer, while his womenfolk cowered in their beds, failed to find an intruder.

Spring came with no more disturbances; summer followed and one of the daughters planned to accompany her mother to a nearby garden party. But mother was not quite ready, so Blanche sat down at the piano to run through a little tune while she waited.

The drawing room door was pushed slightly open and a quiet voice said: "I'm ready now, Blanche."

"Coming mother," Blanche replied, gathering together her music and laying it aside. She left the drawing room, and was in time to see the door at the end of the hall closing. A hand could be seen at the door's edge, but when Blanche followed and went through that door there was nobody on the other side!

Such incidents as these, small though they were, alarmed the women-folk. The farmer, who was quite satisfied with his new property, refused to be upset by them. "I get tired of hearing your nonsense," the girls were told, until one evening when the farmer came back to his home rather later than usual. It was twilight, and a cold evening, and he was surprised to see a woman crouched down by the farm pond, busily rinsing out a sack in the water. Going into the house he was prepared to scold his wife.

"Yon lass is working late," he announced. "You should have more sense than to set her on, with a job like that, at this time-a-day." But a look around the large kitchen where his evening meal was waiting assured him that all his womenfolk were indoors and accounted for.

And so things went on at Peartree Farm. Nobody was interfered with and somehow the family settled down and made the place their home. The occurrences at Peartree Farm seem to be over. A doubting relation took away that stool from the attic, and strange to say the ghosts are laid.

Florence Hopper (1968)

GHOSTLY SPECTRES

DURING the closing years of the 17th century, a former Barnard Castle man, Guy Whitelock, returned to his native town with the strange and exciting rumour that in the castle vault at Bowes was a fortune of buried gold. Whitelock, who had shared the wild exploits of the buccaneers of the Spanish Main, had heard the story while at sea. Now that he was at home once more it seemed that every tavern in Barnard Castle was buzzing with the exciting rumour.

One night Whitelock and a companion, Anthony Garett, were drinking in the old *Punch Bowl* tavern on the Bank, now the historic building known as Blaygroves. They began to talk freely and loudly of the hidden fortune of gold in the castle vault.

"It was while we lay at anchor off the shore of Cuba," Whitelock informed his companion whom he had led into a life of debauchery since they had been at school together. "A young fellow named Tyler of Bowes, with whom I ran away to sea, first mentioned it to me."

"Tell me more about it, Guy," said Garett, and he called the landlord to refill their tankards.

"It all goes back to the time of the Roman occupation," said Whitelock, "when the Roman Legions were being withdrawn from Britain to defend

Rome from the Barbarians, the castle garrison decided to fleece the people before returning home. The villagers were bent on revenge, attacked the castle, but being forewarned, the garrison buried the treasure in the vault. One night the vassals set fire to the castle, and the garrison was overwhelmed and slaughtered to a man. The treasure was never found."

Whitelock reminded Garett that on the anniversary of the garrison's defeat, ghosts of the murdered soldiers were said to perform the ritual of burying the gold. "Anyone with sufficient courage to witness the spectacle will afterwards dig up and seize the spoil."

Garett shuddered. He was younger and weaker in every way than his companion, but they were both desperately in need of money. With the experienced Whitelock in command, the enterprise was at least worth risking.

Whitelock rose to his feet, and said: "An hour to midnight, and a four mile walk to Bowes—."

A storm broke as they trudged along the long Roman road. Lightning flashes illuminated the old fortress, and its foundations seemed to shake as peals of thunder rumbled down the valley of the Greta.

Garett tremblingly clutched his companion's arm. Pieces of mortar which had stood the wear and tear and weather for 800 years fell around them like hail. Suddenly all was calm. The storm passed. A muffled peal rang out the midnight hour. They were still listening to the dying boom of the last stroke when the place was lit by a strange light, and the old fortress emerged in all its former grandeur.

Steel-clad warriors, their armour shining in the light, paced majestically with noiseless tread along the rugged battlements. At a signal from the chief a long procession was formed followed by eight grey-bearded warriors carrying a large chest. They surrounded the spot where Whitelock and Garett stood dumbfounded, almost petrified with fear.

As each ghostly figure strode into the tower, the two frightened men took a tighter grip on their swords. They dared not move until the last of the eight warriors entered and lowered the chest into the deep vault in the north corner. Then a momentary flash made them blink. Suddenly the sky was as black as ever and the storm resumed its former violence.

Garett moved to flee, but Whitelock turned swiftly upon his companion, and killed him with a sword stroke. In a fit of madness he dug down into the earth where he had seen the chest deposited by the phantom soldiers. He toiled on like a maniac until he struck a piece of wood.

A blood-red hand appeared before him. He tried to speak as it beckoned him, waved him on over the body of his companion, and out into the fields and to the edge of the flooded Greta. And away over the

river it still beckoned him, until Whitelock's cries were drowned by the roar of the torrent.

Garett's body was found next day. Two days later searchers found the body of the murderer cast upon the rocks at the point where the rivers meet.

I know quite a number of parsons who believe in ghosts, but I have heard of only one instance of a parson actually talking to a ghost, and this evidently happened at Rokeby, where the Tees and Greta meet, about two centuries ago.

The incident was mentioned by John Morritt, the owner of Rokeby Hall, in a letter to his friend, Sir Walter Scott, about the year 1809. A little while before, Scott had spent some time at Rokeby Hall as Morritt's guest, and his famous poem *Rokeby* was afterwards dedicated to Morritt. Scott vividly described his visit to Teesdale, particularly his walk through the woods to Brignal, and ended his long letter to his friend by requesting information about the legend of the headless lady of Mortham Tower.

Morritt in reply, described the legend in full. The Rokebys, who had come over with William the Conqueror, had held a fortified dwelling at Rokeby until it was destroyed by Scottish raiders in the time of Edward II. After that they had built nearby Mortham Tower, which is now a farm house.

"Several centuries ago," wrote Morritt, "one of the Lords of Rokeby murdered his beautiful young wife in a frenzy of jealousy, suspecting that she was the mistress of one of the Northern Barons. He cut off his wife's head, and threw it into the River Tees. On returning to his home, Mortham Tower, he noticed as he ascended the staircase, that blood

was dropping from his dagger, and the blood stains on the floor were indelible. So it came about that the Tower and places nearby are haunted by the headless ghost of the lady."

Morritt went on to describe the ghost. "She is dressed as a fine lady with a piece of white silk trailing behind her. A parson once by talking to her in Latin confined her under the bridge where the Tees flows past my dairy, but the arch being destroyed by the floods of 1771, became incapable of containing her any longer."

Shortly after the last war, the rector of Rokeby began to investigate the case of the headless lady, after a Mr. and Mrs. Featherston, who live at Mortham Tower, had told him that they had seen the ghost in their bedroom, just as Morritt had described it, "trailing a piece of white silk behind it." They added that their guest, a young Irishman, had also seen it in the same bedroom.

The Rector was so interested that he contacted a representative of *The Northern Echo*, who published an account of the experience.

During the last century another headless ghost was seen from time to time near Hardraw, in Upper Wensleydale. It was the spectre of an old woman.

A short distance from Hardraw stand two dwellings known as Rigg House, originally one large house owned by a sullen and unpopular man

named Metcalfe, known as "Blackwhipper", because he had once been a slave owner. Metcalfe's housekeeper, an old woman, mysteriously disappeared, and shortly afterwards rumours of a headless spectre were reported in the district. Long after Metcalfe had left the district the haunting continued, until the landlord of Rigg House pulled down the middle portion destroying the room where the ghost walked.

On a stretch of road between Aysgarth and Woodhall in Wensleydale, the ghost of an elderly lady in mid-Victorian dress has been seen from time to time in recent years. Witnesses have spoken of her being attired in a crinoline-shaped black dress, coloured hat, white gloves, and with a walking stick in her hand.

Several people claim to have met her, and some have been on the point of speaking to her, but she has vanished. She haunts the same piece of road, about two hundred yards of it, a considerable distance from any house or building with which she might possibly be associated.

In Yorkshire and other northern counties there is a belief in a ghost dog called The Padfoot, about the size of a small donkey, black with shaggy hair and with large eyes like saucers. It follows people about or waylays them in lonely spots, and is regarded as a precursor of death. People say that they have heard it following them, and making a strange padding sound with its paws.

The lane which leads over the hump-backed bridge to Ivelet in Swaledale is reputed to be haunted by the ghost of a black dog whose appearance is always a sign of some tragic event to come. It is said to glide silently on to the bridge, and disappear over the ledge.

This lane may well be haunted since it lies on The Old Corpse Way, which formerly led from Keld at the top of the dale to the ancient church of Grinton. Centuries ago the dead were brought this way for internment. Bearers had a twelve miles walk.

At Ridings Farm, near Blades are the ruins of a barn still known as "The Dead House" where funeral processions used to rest, while the bearers went down for refreshment to *The Punch Bowl* at Fleetham. They usually spent the night there.

Near Rudstone church in the East Riding is a giant monolith which (legend tells) was hurled at the church by the Devil. There is also a belief that the Devil, or one of his disciples, prowls around the graves of those who have lived a none too virtuous life, waiting for an opportunity to whisk away their spirits.

There are numerous legends associated with the Devil in the North Riding. Tradition tells that North Otterington church was originally intended to be built on a hill close to Thornton-le-Moor, but at night the Devil moved the stones to North Otterington. Likewise it was intended to build a church on the top of Borrowby Bank, which commands one of the finest views of the Vale of Mowbray but, legend tells, the Devil shifted the stones at night to Leake, the valley below, where the isolated church still stands.

The three giant stone pillars at Boroughbridge are known as "The Devil's Arrows", and beneath the western slopes of the Hambleton Hills are The Devil's Parlour and The Devil's Highway. On the summit of Hood Hill, nearby, are "the Devil's Footmarks".

One summer's day in the early 1930's, I was toiling up Sutton Bank to the summit of the Hambleton Hills, when an elderly man approached me from an isolated house at the steepest point of the bank.

"Must be very quiet and lonely up here on winter nights. It's the sort of time and place for ghosts," I jokingly said.

The old man gave me a startled glance. "Ghosts," he repeated. "Now it's funny you mentioning ghosts. I saw one here once. It was one night a few years ago, and I was standing right here where I'm now–."

He said he was looking for his dog, which had wandered off down towards Hood Hill, and was just going to cross the road when he saw what looked like a bright light moving up the bank. "I watched for a minute, then crossed the road towards it, and it seemed to be that sort of form of a woman, rather small and thin. Then when I got closer, I felt a cold sort of current of air sweep past me, and the thing had gone."

For a long time afterwards I almost forgot the encounter. Then one August day in 1936 came the news of a very interesting and important discovery on Sutton Bank. Workmen repairing the road unearthed a shallow grave in which was the skeleton of a woman just over five feet in height, and several bronze ornaments and vessels. The burial was dated by archaeologists to about 1400 B.C., and the skeleton is in the museum at Northallerton. The grave, almost directly opposite the house, outside which I was told the ghost story some four or five years before the discovery, is now fenced off, and the contents and discovery are marked by an inscription.

Some time afterwards, I called at the house hoping to find the teller of the ghost story, but was told by the new occupants that he had left some time before. I have often thought of his story since, and his experience impressed me by its remarkable resemblance to other ghost stories I have heard and read since, particularly the teller's reference to experiencing a cold draught of air.

My uncle used to say that a spectral horseman haunted the once famous racecourse on the Hambleton Hills, and a spectral white monk was believed to appear above the steep white crags of Whitestonecliff, just north of the summit of Sutton Bank, to warn travellers of the precipitous drop.

My uncle also used to say that it was believed during his boyhood that the ghost of a witch named Abigail Craister, who had jumped over Whitestonecliff to escape the pursuing hounds during one of the many cruel witch hunts in the district during the reign of James I, appeared from time to time on the edges of Lake Gormire, beneath Whitestonecliff.

William Foggitt (1963)

THE PHANTOM DRIVER

YORKSHIRE has a fair share of ghosts to its credit. One of the most intersting was a "warning ghost", originally a farmer's daughter named Nance. She was betrothed to Tom, a neighbouring farm hand, but just before the wedding she lost her heart to a glib-tongued persuasive stranger from York, and to everybody's surprise – and Tom's dismay – she eloped and married the stranger instead.

In order to assuage his grief, and to try to forget, Tom left the farm where he had been employed, and became a coachman on the route from York to Hull. About a year later, when he was returning to York, to his great surprise he saw Nance sitting in the grass on the roadside nursing a baby.

Recognition was mutual, and she called out to him to stop. When he did so, and had clambered down out of his driver's seat, he found to his great dismay that Nance was dying. He lifted both her and the baby tenderly into the coach, and drove them to a friend's house in York. Then he listened while Nance told her story.

Her husband had turned out to be a highwayman. He already had a wife and family. Nance, heartbroken over her own treatment and repentant over her shabby treatment of Tom, grasped his hand and whispered, "If my spirit is allowed to return, I will always warn you, your childer, and your childer's childer of any coming danger."

Shortly after Nance was laid to rest Tom was sent to Durham to drive four important clients to York on urgent business for the King. They were late in starting off, and urged Tom to get there as quickly as possible, each promising him a guinea if he arrived in York "by eight chimes".

Things ran smoothly and well until the coach was some ten miles out of York, when a thick fog rolled over the countryside, blotting out the road so completely that Tom was forced to draw his horses into a walk. But to his amazement at that very moment a ghostly form took her place by his side and laid her cold hands on the reins.

Tom had no doubt that the ghost was Nance and he handed over the reins without the least hesitation. The ghost urged the horses into a gallop, the guard tootled his horn, and along the fog-shrouded road the sawying coach thundered through the dusk, scattering other travellers and leaving toll-gate keepers agape.

Meanwhile the four startled travellers in the coach became terrified and shouted to Tom to rein in his horses and drive more carefully. "Have no fear, gentlemen!" Tom shouted back. "You are in safe hands, and you'll be in York by eight chimes!"

He was quite right. The coach rattled over York's cobblestones and into the yard of the *Black Swan* just as the clocks were striking eight, and as the four travellers thankfully handed over their guineas to Tom the ghostly form of Nance disappeared in to the fog.

R.W. Hornsey (1960)

AN OLD MANOR HOUSE

CHRISTMAS will soon be upon us, with its presents, its good cheer and those stories of ghosties and ghoulies without which no Christmas would be complete. Here is a ghost story concerning an old Manor House a few miles from Driffield.

It would not be fair to tell you exactly where the house is, for there are children in the family and we don't want to spoil their Christmas holidays. But I have been told the story of little Emily, who weeps up there in the old attics, and her big sister Mary, who long, long ago murdered a tinker and successfully hid his body in the open chimney in one of the guest rooms in that large country house.

The family took their coach and, some few days before the events of which I will tell you, went off to London to spend the festive season at their town house. Mary, the cook, was left in charge, and for company she asked her younger sister, about 14 years old, to come to stay with her. There was no other staff, except old William the gardener, who did not live in the house.

The cook – a healthy robust young woman – took a large kitchen knife and went out into the garden to cut a cabbage. Little Emily busied herself at the kitchen sink. A tinker called at the back door. At first he tried to sell some of his wares to little Emily, but when he realised that she was alone in the house he grew bold, set down his tray and entered the kitchen.

He took the young girl in his arms, but Mary returned and without thought plunged her large knife into the tinker's back.

The tinker fell at her feet. Mary tried to comfort her sister, but when the weeping was stilled Mary found to her horror that she had a dead man on her hands. What should she do with him? At first she thought of calling in old William, but dare they confide in him? Together they could dig a grave and bury the tinker in the garden, but would William hold his tongue?

Mary decided that they could trust no one, and that until she could think of a better idea they would drag the body up into one of the attics. Searching drawers for towels and wrappers to tie about the body and staunch the blood she soon made a heavy parcel of the corpse, while Emily shivered and wept. Then began a tough haul to get their gruesome bundle up the stairs.

By the time they reached the first landing they were both exhausted. Perhaps if Emily had not been in such a state they might well have succeeded, but Mary realised that they could go no further and instead the tinker was taken into the nearest bedroom, where the cook decided he could be hidden until such time as they could deal with him.

In those days they chimneys in the old house were very large and open, fitted with iron loops so that the little chimney sweeps could climb up inside to clear the soot in the spring. To one of these iron loops Mary strung the tinker's body. It was out of sight, there was ventilation, the room was rarely used. It was doubtful if he would ever be found.

One day a smooth, round object rolled into the hearth in that bedroom. It was the tinker's skull. What happened? The chimney in that room was bricked up with the tinker inside. There is no fireplace in that large bedroom today.

I went up to the attics to see the room where little Emily languished and died, for she never recovered from the shock. The wind moaned about the old house, rising to a crescendo at times, dying away to a sigh. It was cold up there and the little hairs on the back of my neck seemed to rise.

I kept looking over my shoulder for I had the feeling that somebody was watching me, and every so often, when a gust of wind buffeted the walls and window, I could hear something. A sigh? A sob? Was it little Emily's ghost?

Florence Hopper (1974)

Part 3

Barguests and Boggarts

THEY WALK THE MOORS

IN THE days before the Industrial Revolution, and for many years after, it was a very serious matter to undertake a journey in Yorkshire, even if that journey was undertaken through comparatively populated parts. Just to go to Bradford with wool, for example, meant packing the load overnight, rising betimes, and after an examination of the horses' feet, preceding the cart on its way, sounding with a staff down the long steep, slippery brow, to find sure footing for the horses, until they should reach the easy going of the rutted main roads.

It was a positive relief when the onset of winter put an end to country travel altogether, because if you went anywhere, you would be up to the saddle-girths in mud. The snow lay so deep and long on the uplands that mail coach passengers were sometimes snowed up for a week, or a fortnight, going over Blackstone Edge, and had to spend Christmas and New Year's Day there, until all the landlord's stock of food at the little inn had been exhausted, and the mail coach travellers had to begin to eat the Christmas presents they were taking to their friends – turkeys, geese and Yorkshire pies.

Yet all Yorkshire folks' objections to travel were not related to the weather, the badness of the roads, or the ease with which the traveller could lose his way and find himself wandering over a trackless waste, as dusk fell, and the will o' the wisp – "Peg's Lantern", as it was called – begin to flit here and there. It was not the perils of this world that travellers feared – though they were there in plenty – but the other-worldly denizens of the moors.

Even the Brontës, who did not travel a great deal, knew all about the

ghosts in their neighbourhood, such as Captain Batt, who walked in Bloody Lane, the lane that led to Oakwell Hall, down which the ghost of Captain Batt had returned unexpectedly to his home on December 9, 1684. In late dusk, he came stalking down the lane through the hall, up the stairs, into his own room, where he vanished, after leaving a bloody footprint. He had been killed that afternoon in a duel in London, just 300 years ago.

Humbler folk than the Haworth parson's family knew of humbler ghosts, such as that of the Scots pedlar, Sandy McLaren. In the closing years of the 18th century, Sandy had supplied the inhabitants of the remote valleys and hills round Ripon with their household wants.

His customers knew, almost to a day, when they might expect him. Then, one Martinmas, he disappeared off the face of the moors. The last customer to admit seeing him alive, an old farmer, had welcomed him as he arrived, and as he did so had seen something in the Scot's face that made him ask quickly how he did.

McLaren admitted that he was sorely troubled in his mind. As he had come across the Gill he had seen the harbinger of death, his wraith, walking to meet him. It was a misty afternoon, and the wraith detached itself from the bank of mist clinging to the hill and moved now close to the packman, now so far away as to be almost out of sight, until finally he had sunk into the ground.

In an hour or so Sandy had recovered his spirits, thanks to the food and drink that the farmer pressed on him, as well as a brisk piece of haggling with his wife over the price of a piece of material for a gown. Refusing an offer of shelter for the night he set off into the gathering dusk. He had a customer to see, he said – a man whom he did not like, and of whom he was afraid, but whom he could handle.

Soon after the disappearance of Sandy a nearby farmer began to show signs of sudden and unaccountable prosperity. His sickly livestock were replaced with newly bought beasts, his buildings repaired, while at his "meal suppers" the table groaned with roast beef, plum pudding, and strong ale. The highlight of the entertainment at those suppers was "guizing". One night the young guizers decided to give a play – about a pedlar who had his pack stolen.

Just when the merriment was at its height an unexpected addition to the cast appeared. The old pedlar, his blue bonnet pulled down over his fleshless brows, his plaid thrown round his shoulders, stalked across the room. The guests ran screaming out of the farmhouse, and henceforth shunned their host, who died in extreme penury.

Yet there were many who would have preferred to meet the pedlar's ghost than some other visitants to the moors. Boggarts occupied a strangely ambivalent position between purely beneficial spirits, such as the fairies, and completely malevolent ones. At his best, the boggart was a kind of hobgoblin, a creature who liked to play pranks, which were not always amusing to those who had to suffer them.

The household of a farmer called Gilbert Gilbertson had been infiltrated by a boggart. Nobody ever saw the spirit, which made its presence felt in no uncertain way, snatching the bowls of bread and milk from the children, or dashing their "butties" from their hands. Sometimes the curtains of their beds would be shaken backwards and forwards, or a heavy weight would press on them in bed and nearly suffocate them.

There was a cupboard, formed by a wooden partition, on the kitchen stairs, and a large knot hole had been left in the planks. These knot holes, called "elf bores", play a large part in Norse folklore, from which much Yorkshire folk belief is drawn. It is said that those who look through them see what they would not.

One day the farmer's youngest boy, in play, pushed a shoe horn into the hole. It was immediately hurled out again, and struck the boy on the hand. It thereupon became a daily practice for the children to play with the boggart in this way, pushing in the horn, to have it shot out again, like a bullet out of a gun.

Terrified at what might be the outcome of this, the farmer's wife prevailed on her husband to quit the farm and leave it to the boggart. As he followed the last load of goods out of the farmyard, a neighbour accosted him. "Well, George, and so you are leaving the old house at last." A deep voice from the bottom of the milk churn replied: "Aye, we're flitting!" It was the boggart. Realising that it was hopeless to try to fly from his persecutor, Gilbertson turned the horse's head and led him back to the farmhouse.

Yet the boggart could abandon his role of playful Brownie or Hobgoblin and appear in much more sinister guise, verging into the Barguest, which will be described in a moment. The boggart might appear in dog form, large, black, or white, with huge padded feet, shaggy hair and gigantic staring eyes.

The boggart which enjoyed the greatest fame in Yorkshire was probably the "boggart of Bunting Nook", a place in Borton, near Sheffield, where three roads met. This boggart was so notorious that mothers terrified their children into good behaviour by threatening to take them to meet him.

If there was a characteristically Yorkshire visitant, it was the Barguest. This was very much a spirit in animal form. It could be a dog of supernatural size and terrifying appearance, or else it could come in the form of a bear, a mastiff dog or any other animal. When in a playful mood, the Barguest could play pranks on those it met.

One barguest was called "The Picktree Brag", and it appeared in the form of a Galloway nag, not an uncommon beast in Yorkshire at this time. One farmer, coming home from market and evidently full of Dutch courage, even mounted the Picktree Brag and rode it part of the way home. It carried him very quietly till it came to a great pond and then it pitched him in, over its head, and trotted away laughing.

It was only very occasionally that barguests were disposed to be so playful. Usually they came as harbingers of approaching death. Only

those soon about to die could see them, but if you touched a companion, he would instantly experience the same vision as yourself. To go out to look for a barguest, instead of seeing it accidentally, was to court instant death, as opposed to one in the near future.

As lately as 1881, a man at Appletreewick went out to confront the barguest of Trollers Gill. Next morning his body was found by shepherds, with such marks inflicted on it as could have been made by no mortal creature. Boggarts and barguests alike seem to have been drawn to spots where the lines of psychic force converged, spots which also served the everyday purpose of crossroads.

While on the road, it was very unpleasant to meet a witch. She could read your mind, she knew your past and future, and she would probably cast a spell on you, or use her powers to kill your loved ones, or your cattle. While travelling at least, witches preferred to wear a mantle which covered the whole body, all of red, with a red hood. This was exactly the same costume as that worn by the fairies, but they were ever so much smaller.

At the sight of a witch it was necessary to clutch your amulet, something that destroyed her power over you. This might be a stone with a natural hole in it, but a more effective amulet was something that belonged to the unburied dead, usually a rag cut from the clothing of a gibbeted malefactor.

Headless women were another characteristically Yorkshire manifestation. At Deadman's Lane, near Greystones, Ecclesall, in Sheffield, a headless woman robed in white appeared from time to time, while another haunted a house at Rotherham, walking down the stairs at midnight, with her head beneath her arm.

Students of folklore have attempted to connect the headless ghosts of Flamborough and innumerable other Yorkshire localities, with the dreaded guillotine of Halifax. "Execution by beheading." says Mrs. Gaskell, "was performed in a summary way upon either men or women who were guilty of but very slight crimes." She professes to believe that the dread of decapitation had left a permanent effect on the minds of inhabitants of the Brontë country.

If headless female ghosts really were the products of the "Halifax gibbet" then we here have the explanation of the proverb that has puzzled so many: "From Hell, Hull and Halifax, good Lord deliver us".

Old Tabby, the Brontës' nurse, complained of the change that had come over Yorkshire, just in her lifetime. Why she had known folk who had seen the fairies sporting by the beck on moonlight nights! "It wur the factories," she said, "as had driven them away!"

Folk beliefs themselves have vanished, but their spirit lives on in the pages of the Brontës. They were able to distil, in their books, the feeling that animated old Tabby's stories – a feeling of darkness, and terror brooding over the moors.

Carson I.A. Ritchie (1984)

HAVE YOU EVER SEEN THE GHOST DOG?

I HAVE seen a "gytrash"! I do not believe in ghosts. I do not believe in a spiritual survival after death. If anyone told me they had seen a "gytrash" I should be inclined to disbelieve them, but still I repeat my opening sentence – I have seen a "gytrash"!

It is twenty-five years ago since I saw it. When my father was alive we used to walk to Ilkley and back twice every week-end; the weather had to be very bad indeed to debar us from our project. On this particular Sunday my father (perhaps better known as Bob Stubbs, the author and originator of Bob Stubbs, Comic Yorkshire Almanac), was prevented from accompanying me on account of an attack of gout. It was a dull damp, dreary sort of a day when I left our house at Idle about half-past one in the afternoon.

Going by way of Baildon Moor and Dick Hudson's I eventually reached the edge of the moor overlooking Ilkley. Rain had fallen heavily during the previous night, making the path over the moor very wet and boggy, consequently I decided that instead of dropping into the town I would turn off to the right in the direction of the "Cow and Calf" and thence by way of Burley Woodhead and Hawksworth.

Very few people were about on such a miserable day and it was not until I got within about half a mile of Hawksworth that I came across my "gytrash" standing in the middle of the road.

This "it" was; quite plain – a big black dog. Whenever I come across a strange dog I always try to get on friendly terms straight away. I snapped my fingers and thumb, at the same time inviting the animal towards me. I was within about ten yards of "it" when it happened.

The dog just disappeared. It neither walked away nor ran – it vanished.

I shall never forget the terror which came over me. I went all over "goose lumps". I snatched my cap from off my head and ran (never slackening speed) until I got into Hawksworth village, where I almost ran into four ladies who were standing talking just round the corner by the graveyard. I stopped and started conversing with them. I don't know what I said but I felt I must talk – I was scared. On arriving home I related my experience to my father and mother and a few friends who were having tea with us. It was suggested that in future I should "take more water with it".

The sequel happened some months after, again while walking over the moor in the direction of Ilkley. I overtook a gentleman, and after passing the time of day our conversation turned to personal matters. He told me that he worked in one of Bradford's largest stores and after closing on Saturday nights he used to set off to Burley Woodhead where he and another three fellows had a camp.

There they stayed until Sunday night, three of them going in the direction of Leeds, whilst my informer set off back to Bradford. In those days the shops did not close as early as they do to-day, and it struck me that my new-found friend would have a very lonely walk alone after ten o'clock at night. I asked him if he ever felt timid on such a lonely road after dark. No; he was not scared of anything on two legs, not with such an ash plant as he carried, but giving a slight chuckle, he admitted that he used to keep his eyes open on the off chance of coming across the "gytrash".

Naturally my curiosity was aroused and I encouraged him to tell me more. He told me that the farmer from whom they rented their camping ground had warned him to be on the look out for the "gytrash" whenever he was travelling along the Hawksworth-Burley Woodhead road.

I felt a cold shiver begin to creep up my spine, and by the time he had finished telling me that the object of which he spoke took the form of a "big black dog", I began to feel those "goose lumps" coming over me again.

I well remember the look of astonishment on the fellow's face when I gasped out the information that I'd seen it. I related my experience.

On parting we exchanged cards, he promising that if ever he came across "it" he would write me, giving a detailed account of the meeting.

It would perhaps have been a more thrilling and interesting conclusion had I been able to chronicle the fact that I duly received the letter in fulfilment of his promise, but I never heard from him, and although I have walked over the moors scores of times since, I have never had the pleasure of renewing his acquaintanceship.

Maybe others have either seen or heard about this "gytrash". I wonder.

Philip R. Saville (1940)

TROLLS ARE BACK IN THE YORKSHIRE DALES

MY SMALL daughter bought a troll. It is a hideous little creature with long strawy hair which she combs continually. The shop where it was obtained had dozens of trolls and weird variations on the troll theme. The gonks were all head but with tiny legs protruding from an almost shapeless mass.

As I looked at them I could understand why superstitious folk in the Yorkshire Dales years ago should be fearful of the wee folk of the underworld: of creatures that went bump in the potholes and caves which honeycomb a large stretch of the Pennines.

The intensive exploration of our caves and potholes during the past century has gradually stripped the underworld of its sense of mystery. When potholers squeezed their way underground with lamps, cameras and surveying instruments many of the systems were hastily vacated by the trolls, fairies, boggarts and witches who had lived here for centuries – according to old tales told by people who did not venture far enough underground to prove or disprove the stories.

Look through a list of Yorkshire underground systems, and you find traces of the wee folk of long ago in such names as Bull Pot of the Witches, Trollers Gill, Fairy Holes, Boggarts Roaring Holes, and a host more.

It is reasonable to suppose that the trolls came to these parts with the Norse settlers of over 1000 years ago, for the troll was a creation of the Scandinavian imagination. He was a cave dweller who wandered about at night, but not so far from home that he would not slip back before the break of a new day. A troll caught out-of-cave in daylight was turned into stone.

The King of the Trolls presided over a subterranean palace adorned by stalactites and (so the story went) large numbers of valuable jewels. Accounts differ as to the appearance of a troll because there were several varieties. One writer described the troll as a swarthy little creature with a huge head, green eyes, and bird's feet attached to stumpy legs.

I have seen models of trolls – genuine old pieces from Scandinavia and not trolls mass-produced to meet a sudden, big, inexplicable demand for them. There were a skov-troll from Norway, an ugly, almost repulsive creation in wood, and a Danish troll with an impish rather than malicious look about him. Apparently the trolls became more malicious the farther north you travelled. Country folk were constantly plagued by them. On the other hand, when there was some misfortune it was useful to have a scapegoat. If there was a fire, or a pail of milk was overturned, there must surely have been a troll in the district.

A narrow, steep-sided limestone ravine called Trollers Gill appears to have been the main centre of troll activity in the Dales. Was their precise home the "swallow" called Hell Hole above Skyreholme Dam? It opens into a large oblong chamber, and members of the Yorkshire Ramblers' Club were down it in June, 1896. No trolls were discovered.

Trolls are big business today. Most fancy goods shops stock them, and the price ranges from a few shillings to £3. One Yorkshire firm took some trolls to the Great Yorkshire Show two years ago. They were intended simply as decoration for a trade stand. So many people showed such interest in them that scores of trolls were sold, a message having been sent hurriedly back to the main shop for further supplies. A horror of one age has become the toy of another.

The genuine wild troll would appear to be extinct in the Dales today, for I have visited several possible old haunts after dark without seeing one. To my knowledge, no potholer has brought one back alive or dead.

Fairies lived in the Dales. Upper Wharfedale has its Fairy Hole, described by Harry Speight as "a low opening in the limestone which can only properly be entered by such tiny sprites as the fairies. Ordinary mortals must descend to an access on all fours." When Speight visited nearby Cove Hole one autumn evening, and entered the cavern, he found "the gaunt and almost complete skeleton of a horse ... My first impulse was that the fairies must be playing their little tricks, but on secondary consideration it was evident that some mischievous wights of larger growth had dragged the bleached frame of bones to the far opening of the cave, intending no doubt to startle human intruders."

The courting couple who walked near Hurtle Pot, in Chapel-le-Dale, one evening, were local people who no doubt knew about the boggart, which was supposed to live at the bottom of the broad 58 feet gash in the limestone. They may have heard that this boggart had a habit of drowning people in the 20 feet deep pool.

They were quite unprepared for the unearthly noises which suddenly arose from the tree-shaded pothole. The two visitors fled in terror. Not long afterwards a man clambered from Hurtle Pot, and made his way back to Weathercote House, where he was staying with the Metcalfe family. He was carrying a flute and, like Orpheus, he had been playing in the underworld!

The tale was jotted down by a traveller named Walter White, who heard that "in olden times the boggart's deeds were terrible, but of late years he only frightened people with noises. Both this and Jingle Pot are choked with water from subterranean channels in flood time, and then there is heard such an intermittent throbbing, gurgling noise, accompanied by what seems dismal gaspings, that a timorous listener might easily believe the boggart was drowning his victims."

When did the witches leave the caves in Easegill which are still associated with them by name? There were no witches there in 1820, when a correspondent of the *Lonsdale Magazine* arrived in the district, for he assured "the timid reader" that all the witches "which formerly haunted this dirty, gloomy cavern are either dead or banished to the Highlands of Scotland, where they frequently cross the path of a Scott or a Hogg."

He asked a local man about the name of the caves, and was told: "I never sa' any witches, but me grandmuddar said at a parshall a witches ust to meet yance a ear e thor hoals, an mead a girt feast, an neabody mud gang tull it, but sic as thersels."

The old writer was correct when he stated that Easegill's Witches' Caves are dirty and gloomy. In the entrance to one of them he wrote: "To the right we found a pool of water, to the left a pool of mud, and in the middle a mixture of both. This cave is nothing but creaks and crannies among the loose strata of the limestone." He lamented that the witches had left the place full of water!

From the Witches' Caves, at river level, to Casterton Fell, where there is another gash in the limestone which has associations with the "women in black" – Bull Pot of the Witches, 210 feet deep. The Balderstons, of Ingleton, visiting Bull Pot in 1888, found it was "a dreadful hole, foetid with the dead carcasses of sheep and lambs, and whitened with skeletons. A vast cave-like mouth is to be seen in the base of its north-western side."

A name they gave to Leck Fell's Rumbling Hole is "The Fairies' Work-shop", and they added: "But hark! tap, tap, tap, comes slowly from the distant depths; this is the home of the gnomes or fairies; they are at work below in their workshop, and a far-off hammering can be heard. Leave them in peace! Some day the good fays may work your weal, although the ill-natured have designated as Rumbling Hole what we prefer to dream of as The Fairies' Workshop."

Folk lore is usually lost, or forgotten, and seldom is it destroyed. Yet potholers who went to Robin Hood's Mill, near Stainforth, in North Ribblesdale before the last war, were blamed for stopping some old grindstones from turning deep in the earth! The shaft, near the river, had been known as the "Mill" for generations, and a local legend stated that a mill once stood here, the owner of which, not content with making a great deal of money during the week, once kept his grindstone turning on the Sabbath Day.

As a punishment for his breach of the Commandment, the mill sank out of sight, and a low murmuring sound which came from the sink-hole was said to be the noise of the mill-stones still grinding away. Before the potholers began their exploration they were warned by a clergyman that in trying to solve the mystery they might destroy the romance associated with it.

The potholers excavated the hole to a depth of 10 ft. to 12 ft., and the rumbling sound was then to be heard. Later the rumbling ceased, and it was believed that debris was interposed between the sound from below and the ear of the listener. It had been muffled rather than stopped.

Many potholers, breaking into what they considered to be new sys-tems, and pushing excitedly through caverns which have apparently been untouched by hand, have been humbled to discover that "t'Owd Man" has been there before them. "T'Owd Man" is a collective name for past generations of lead-miners, and signs of his presence in a system have been the discovery of broken clay pipes, old candles, and piles of refuse dislodged in the unending search for lead.

The lead-miners were a superstitious lot. A group of men who have been exploring the lead-mines of Greenhow and Swaledale have dis-covered luck-stones – stones with holes in the middle, threaded with string, which "t'Owd Man" liked to hang in the areas where he was working.

Does the ghost of "t'Owd Man" still wander on the heights of Greenhow? A member of the Cave Study Group was camping by the hut at Stump Cross one night when there was a full moon aloft. He heard the sound of clogs coming down the road about midnight and left his car to investigate. The sound came nearer, passed him and went towards Greenhow village. There was no-one about.

Perhaps "t'Owd Man" still walks on moonlit nights. No one in recent times has reported seeing a troll or fairy, or a boggart or witch, in these limestone areas, possibly because no one in these sophisti-cated, scientific times, ever thinks of looking for them. But, hush – what was that?

B.T. Frankland (1966)

A GLAISDALE HOB

OLD books tell the story of the Hob of Hart Hall, Glaisdale, whom they describe as a shaggy hard-working little fellow. Every night while the farmer slept he would be busy in the barn threshing the corn with his flail. And every morning the farmer would find the grain threshed and winnowed.

Baffled, he kept watch to try and discover the identity of his unpaid helper – and he did, but it was his undoing. For what he saw was a small unkempt brown personage without any clothes, and in an effort to reward him for his toil he presented the fellow with a tunic.

The clothing was made from coarse hemp, and this offended the little goblin. His objection was not to the offer of clothing from a benevolent farmer, but the quality of the material of which it was made.

The people from Hart Hall, while anxious to prevent the hob from catching cold, did not think it worth-while to consider his feelings in the manner of dress. The right thing for them to have done was to have provided him with a green suit on the pattern worn by the local fairies.

As it was, the vexed goblin refused their gift, snapping: "Gin Hob mun ha'e nowt but a hardin hamp. He'll come nae mair nowther to berry nor stamp." (If Hob can have nothing but a hardin tunic then he can come no more to thresh the corn.) Hob departed and, true to his word, was never seen again.

(1971)

Part 4

Here and There

THEY EXTERMINATED MONSTERS

WHEN the Brothers Grimm set down the tale *Jack the Giant-killer*, they were epitomising a universal theme – man's triumph over monster, typifying the victory of good over evil. Yorkshire and its neighbouring counties have many stories of those who vanquished wild boars, bears and wolves; of serpents, giants and even "Saracens". Monstrous "worms" are a speciality in these parts, although anything larger than an adder would be foreign to the region. Do these stories stem from Scandinavian myth ? Or the tradition of St. Hild?

Three stories of worm-slaying come to mind and the best-known is probably that of the Lambton Worm, a creature said to have terrorised the countryside around Chester-le-Street. The worm made its lair on a hillock near the home of the Lambtons until one of them went boldly up and slew it, using for the purpose a falchion belonging to the family.

An almost identical tale is told of a Conyers of Sockburn-on-Tees who delivered that vicinity from a great worm; he used the family's falchion to do so, and this weapon is exhibited in the library at Durham cathedral. It used to be presented annually to the Prince-Bishops of Durham as a token rent. The same could have been true of the Lambton blade. This crude Dunelmian ditty has secured the perpetuation of the Lambton myth:

'Whisht, lads, o'd yah gobs,
Ah'll tell ye a' an a'fu' story
Whisht, leads, o'd yan gobs,
Ah'll tell ye 'bout that worrrm.'

The third of the worm-slayers is different in that for him no claim is made for knightly descent. He is simply called "Scaw". His worm haunted a wood near Handale abbey, close by Loftus, on the northern edge of the Cleveland hills.

Handale, be it noted, had connections with Whitby Abbey. Today the site of the nunnery is occupied by a farm. The building housing the nuns was made into a linen mill in Napoleonic times, and later collapsed under the weight of machinery.

The Scandinavian *orm* is translated "snake or serpent", and could be used to infer any great reptile. Orm was popular as a name for men, so that it is possible that we have here the story of the killing of a menacing Norseman. The name "Scaw" has been associated with the nearby Scawood, but *skaw* (shaw) comes from a Norse word meaning a wood that has been reduced by the felling of trees. Shaw is a family name well-known from the Humber to the Highland line. Scaw's worm, which made its home in a cave, was finicky about its diet, aiming to live exclusively on the flesh of young maidens. As it continued to deplete the region, Scaw arrived with the appropriate falchion and, after a tough contest, was proved the winner. His prize was an earl's daughter whom he rescued from the cave and, of course, married.

Another monster which frequented a wood was a man-eating giant. Feeble embellishments have distorted this figure, giving him "legs like an elephant's", not a likely simile for a medieval story-teller; "one eye in the middle of his forehead" – culled from the Cyclops tale; and "no clothing except a cow-hide draped across his chest" – clearly based on memories of John Baptist. In truth he is a woodhouse, a wild man of the woods, or greenman. He based himself in Sessay Wood, near Topcliffe, which was then tenanted by a Darrel family. Joan Darrel vowed that she would marry whoever killed the woodhouse.

The time came when the giant was tobbing a mill – there was an affinity between giants and mills – and a change of wind brought the sails round to fell him to the ground. Guy d'Aunay (Dawney), happening to be on hand, snatched up a miller's pick and administered the coup which won him the lady. Poor wild man! He probably represents some oddity of society, unjustly maligned and forced to take to a predatory existence. He cannot be said to have perished in fair fight.

Dragons presented special problems. Their hides were scaly and warty – well-nigh impenetrable. They were armoured with iron-hard teeth and claws, were very active in spite of their vast bulk, could use necks and tails as supporting weapons and, above all, had foul breath or fire to assail disturbers. Many were credited with a kind of E.S.P. and most of them possessed secret powers of resuscitation. Call them ancestral memories, or rate them as left-overs from the age of reptiles, they were not to be ignored, particularly when they developed an appetite for maidens and children. Monsterwise they lurked on small hills – probably ancient occupation sites. Not surprisingly some of the stories about dragon-fighting include the provision of purpose-built armour and the use of supernatural charms to protect their heroes. Two tales, one from Yorkshire and the other from Lancashire, tell of champions wearing "anti-dragon harness".

Near East Newton stands Loschy Hill, on which lived a sinuous brute – wyvern or serpent – which smothered its victims in its coils, attacking with teeth and claws when that failed. A challenger was found in a certain Peter Loschy, who wore a harness covered all over with razor-blades. He set off for the combat accompanied by his dog. The encounter began with the dragon winding its coils about the knight, but as the blades bit it soon released its hold. Peter, able to attack with his sword, hacked at the beast, yet, much as he wounded it, its hurts were mended immediately. At last he managed to slash a strip from the whole length of its side. The dog darted in and dragged this away for a distance of about a furlong. When a second such strip was cut off, the hound took that away in the opposite direction. Gradually pieces were slashed off and distributed to all points of the compass until nothing remained except the head still snapping, spitting and snarling.

Despite the danger the brave animal seized even this by the corner of its jaw, and transported it, too. As Loschy stood gasping and trembling on the hill, the dog returned with wagging tail. His master knelt to fondle him, and the dog licked his face. Thus both were contaminated by the poison of the dragon and fell dead where they had triumphed. In Nunnington church is the effigy of a knight who is almost certainly Sir William de Tayes, although local inhabitants insist that it is Peter Loschy who is commemorated.

The Lancashire parallel was the Dragon of Wantley. This so persecuted the neighbourhood that at last the villeins went as a body to a (fictitious) knight called "More" of More Hall to demand deliverance. After some demurring, the knight went off to Sheffield, where he had made for himself a harness studded all over with spikes. His combat with the Worm was going badly for him until he happened to kick it in the middle of the back. This proved to be a vulnerable spot and the foe succumbed immediately.

At Long Witton a dragon established itself in one of three health-giving wells, giving no offence so long as people kept away from the wells. For the locality to be denied the waters was intolerable. A knight errant – no name is given – undertook to remove the intruder. It so happened that the dragon could render itself invisible, a significent point, but the knight possessed an ointment which, applied to the eyes, gave him the power of seeing the invisible. The details of this contest are long. Briefly, the dragon was able to heal its wounds and renew its strength by keeping the tip of its tail in the well. After several days of renewed attack the knight realised what was happening. Accordingly he lured the dragon away from the water and was able to accomplish its slaughter.

Guy was not the only Dawnay in the business. Another one, Sir William, accompanied Richard Lionheart on the Crusade, coming thus to Acre. The story goes that he "killed the chief Prince of the Saracens." It must have gone hard with the latter, who is recorded as having been slain by numerous champions. Sir William later distinguished himself by slaying a "lion". There could be some confusion here. Many of the Saracen leaders had soubriquets like "the Falcon", "the Tiger" and "the Lion". Maybe the leader killed by Sir William was one such as these, or it could be that he had two victims. In any case the story goes on to say that King Richard gave Dawnay a massive silver ring set with a talismanic "toad-stone", and also awarded him a crest – a demi-Saracen in armour with a ring in one hand and a lion's paw in the left hand – in perpetual memory of the dead. The crest cannot be disputed, but crests were not invented until a later time in history.

A most puzzling tale exists regarding a hero of the family of Stapylton, of Wighill. He is said to have exterminated a Saracen who lived "on an island off the coast of England." A whole set of confusions may be involved here. One remembers immediately that over a long period of time the Island of Lundy was held by a pirate family named Marisco against all comers. Saracen pirates did raid along our coasts. They could have formed alliances with local outlaws. A simpler explanation could be that any stranger – especially a dark-skinned one – might be dubbed "Saracen". To find "an island off the coast of North East England" Stapylton would have had to go to the Farne Islands.

All these stories contain a common element in that the hero is destroying a menace. A menace might be anything unfamiliar, dangerous or otherwise. Just as the *Book of Daniel* and the *Book of Revelations* are cryptic histories of struggles against tyranny, so our folk-lore tells of terrors withstood and wickedness defeated. Twrch Trwyth, the gigantic wild boar overcome by the hero Kilwych in Welsh legend, was something other than a pig, but the story, disseminated by popular recital could have produced others, such as the slaying of the wild boar of

Kentmere by William Gilpin. On the other hand we may have here the history of Man's struggle to establish himself in the face of difficulties. Modern conservationists can hardly fail to detect in them the early records of the process by which, in making England safe for heroes to live in, man has exterminated his competitors.

G.E. Pallant-Sidaway (1972)

LEGENDS FROM A BOWLAND VILLAGE

THERE are two streams in Bolton-by-Bowland – Kirkbeck (running by the church) and Skirden (a tributary of the Ribble). Our Northern streams quickly rise and fall. There was a ford across the Skirden about a mile below the village which was used by the wagons and carts visiting Bolton Hall. I remember a flood at this ford which washed away a wagon and three horses and fifty-two sacks of corn. The wagoner got safely across because he was riding the foremost horse.

Pendle Hill is plainly visible from the village. This great peak was made famous by the Lancashire witches who were supposed to ride over on broomsticks, and as children we always thought the witches were in the air when we heard the bats cry on summer evenings.

The family of Pudsay were the owners of Bolton Hall for many generations; they were great Royalists, and sheltered Henry VI after the battle of Hexham in 1464. They were also good churchmen, and one of the most remarkable monuments in the church is a huge flat slab of limestone with figures in bas-relief of Sir Ralph Pudsay, his three wives and twenty-five children. Some are in armour, some dressed as priests, and the women are in the Elizabethan coifs of their day.

There were all sorts of stories and legends about the Pudsay family. One who lived at the hall at the time of Queen Elizabeth (she was said to be his godmother) was fond of entertaining his friends. In this way he spent all the fortune he possessed. He did not know where to find the money to pay his debts.

He consulted two elves – Lob and Michael – who were supposed to live in a cave in the woods which surrounded Bolton Hall, and these told Pudsay he must go to a certain lead mine on his Bolton property, where he would find a vein of silver. He followed their advice, set up a mint at the Water Mill, and minted his own silver shillings to pay his debts.

The authorities at York heard of this, and sent soldiers to capture Pudsay and take him to prison. But his good friends, Lob and Michael, had presented Pudsay with a magical silver bit and told him that if this bit was in the mouth of his horse it would never tire. Directly the report reached him that the soldiers were near he rushed out, put the bit in the horse's mouth, the saddle on its back, and rode off to the woods. There was a big cliff in the woods, the river flowing at its foot, over 100 feet below. Pudsay is reported to have said: "Better a leap from my own grey rock, than from the gallows at York." The magic of the bit saved the horse. It came down without bend of knee and Pudsay was able to ride on to London. Queen Elizabeth was on her barge in the Thames, but undismayed he made his horse swim out to the barge and we, as children, thought him very hard-hearted when he turned to his horse and said: "Shift for yourself, my gallant grey."

A.C. Fowle (1952)

TRAIL OF THE WHITE DOE

I FIRST heard about the White Doe on a visit to the old *Shoulder of Mutton* inn at Blackshaw Head, high up in the hills above Hebden Bridge and Todmorden. Ken Evans, a friend and colleague, had recently been there painting a mural based on a local legend and had now returned with his family to apply the finishing touches. My family and I had gone along for the outing.

The mural shows the hall of a large and ancient residence. In the centre, with attendants looking on, stands a nobleman with a captive white doe which was obviously terrified of the yelping dogs that are threatening to attack. Alongside the mural is a brief resume of the legend, explaining the events in the picture. Long ago, it says, the beautiful Lady Sybil lived at Bernshaw Tower. She loved to walk to the Eagle's Crag and would often stand there gazing into the wooded chasm beneath and longing for the supernatural power of a witch.

Eventually, the narrative continues, she bartered her soul to the devil in return for the magic power to change her shape, whereupon she would roam the hills in the form of a white doe. Lord William Towneley of Hapton Tower, sought the help of Mother Helston, a famous local witch who advised him that if he wanted to catch the milk-white beast, he must seek it in the gorge of Cliviger. One day, while hunting there, he chased and caught it. In triumph he led the beautiful animal back to Hapton Tower. Next morning however, Lady Sybil had returned to her human form. She soon renounced witchcraft and married Lord William!

Such was the story as far as it went. I was fascinated. Here were the makings of a story of mystery and romance. What basis had it in history, I wondered, and what had become of the places mentioned in the legend? As a stranger to the district (although Yorkshire-bred I now live in Cheshire), I had to start from scratch.

Tentative local enquiries that day got me no further than establishing the general direction in which Eagle's Crag lay, and the fact that Hapton Tower was somewhere in the Burnley area. The next step was to try to fill in the details of the story, find out something about the main characters, and pinpoint the main scenes of action. A couple of months later in the late autumn, the opportunity arose for Ken and I to return to Blackshaw Head – on our own this time – to browse around, getting the feel of the place and seeing what fresh information we could gather. Without a map of the area and following the vaguest of directions, we set out to try to find Eagle's Crag. We took the car as far as we could along a moorland road and then struck off across country, heading for a group of rocks on the skyline. By then it was late afternoon and although the sky was clear, the wind was strong and biting, and the ground hard and snow-flecked. Eventually we sought the shelter of the rocks, only to realise that this was not Eagle's Crag but the grotesquely-shaped Bottle Neck near the Great Bride Stones. (Eagle's Crag, as we were to discover later, lay on the other side of the Cliviger gorge!) We returned at dusk to Hebden Bridge Public Library.

In the local history section here I discovered corroboration of the story. In T.T. Wilkinson's *Ancient Mansions near Burnley, their History and Owners*, Bernshaw Tower was described as having been a small fortified house which, at the time of writing (a hundred years or so ago), "was in ruins, with very little else than the foundations visible above the surface!" It stood, said the author, in one of the beautiful ravines, branching off from the great gorge of Cliviger, five miles from Burnley. According to the writer, Lady Sybil was an heiress, celebrated for her wealth and beauty, and she had been the last owner of Bernshaw Tower. Forthermore, she was "intellectual beyond most of her sex." Wilkinson's story agrees on her visits to Eagle's Crag and adds that she attested the bond with the devil in her blood in order that she might join the nightly revels of the Lancashire witches. He mentions that at the period in question, Hapton Tower was the home of a junior branch of the Towneley family and "Lord William" had for long been a suitor for the hand of Lady Sybil, but always in vain. He went to Mother Helston because he had heard of Lady Sybil's escapades as a doe. After resorting to spells and incantations she eventually promised him his desire on the next All Hallows Eve.

Once the doe had been spotted near the crag, the chase was long and arduous, and the hounds were near exhaustion when, as they returned towards Eagle's Crag, another hound appeared which Lord William recognised. Mother Helston had sent it to catch the doe. Disaster almost overcame Lord William when his horse, passing the crag, reared and nearly threw its rider into the valley below. However, just as the doe was about to leap on the next rock, the mysterious hound seized it by the neck, holding it until Lord William could throw an enchanted silken cord round its neck to lead the beautiful animal back to Hapton Tower.

According to this account, the tower shook that night as in an earthquake before Lady Sybil was found restored to her natural form. At this point the two versions differ. While the *Shoulder of Mutton* version seems to imply a life of wine and roses ever after, Mr. Wilkinson has a very different tale to tell. After a year of married life Lady Sybil could abstain from her former practices no longer. One night, having assumed the form of a white cat, she was frolicking in the Cliviger mill when Robin, a manservant, cut off one of her paws with his whittle. The following morning, Lady Sybil lay in her bed at Hapton Tower, pale and exhausted.

However, her sudden indisposition was soon explained when Robin arrived bearing a lady's hand. Lord William had no difficulty recognising its owner by its signet ring, and expressed his anger at his wife's relapse in no uncertain terms. However, by some magic process the hand was restored to Lady Sybil's arm, although a red ring at her wrist remained to bear evidence of the blade's sharpness. Happily, a reconciliation was achieved, but Lady Sybil's health and strength ebbed away. Shortly before she died, with the help of the local clergy, the devil's bond was cancelled so that Lady Sybil could die in peace. According to local tradition, her body was buried at the foot of the Eagle's Crag, since when, every All Hallow's Eve a ghostly hound and a milk-white doe meet a spectral hunt in full chase on the crag. Such then, was the tale I found at Hebden Bridge that evening. It was too late to take matters further immediately but here was ample food for thought. When did this strange happening take place? Who exactly were "Lord William" and "Lady Sybil"? Would the locations tell us anything more?

My next move was to pinpoint Eagle's Crag, Hapton Tower, Cliviger Mill and the rest, on six-inch O.S. maps in Manchester reference library. Following Wilkinson's clues I soon found what I was looking for on the map of the Cliviger gorge through which now runs the A646 between Todmorden and Burnley. Eagle's Crag was about a mile outside Todmorden towering 300 feet above the road, and here, a mile or so nearer Burnley, slightly higher than the crag, was marked "Bernshaw" Tower, situated on the edge of Tower Clough and above Tower Wood. Then, as I traced the gorge westwards I realised what might well have had profound implications for the whole background to the story – that although Bernshaw Tower and Eagle's Crag lay in Yorkshire, the border with Lancashire was only a thousand yards or so to the west! Here was a new dimension to the tale, an independent-minded Yorkshirewoman receiving the attentions of a young Lancastrian nobleman! Significantly too, the flat hill-top area above Bernshaw Tower was marked as Deerplay Moor. Cliviger Mill, I found, was further west, out of the gorge proper, at the rear of Townley Park. After considerable searching I eventually located the site of Hapton Tower in Hapton Park, 1½ miles or so south of Burnley and west of the A56. According to Wilkinson, Hapton Park was enclosed by Sir John Towneley, who lived in the days of Queen

Elizabeth. The park had walls ten miles in circumference, although little
of these still remain. The tower, which was inhabited until 1667, had
also been demolished.

With rough sketch maps made of the relevant areas I was now ready
to visit the locations. The first opportunity for a return trip came the
following January. The weather was not exactly ideal for exploration,
with grey skies and a light snow covering on the hills, but it was by
no means hopeless. Having lunched early in Hebden Bridge, we were
driving back along the A646 towards Cliviger, looking for Bernshaw
Tower's site, when we spotted Eagle's Crag, high above us on the left.
There was no mistaking it with the aquiline head and wing jutting out
to give the impression of the "king of birds" in flight. Later we were to
return to the rock, but for the time being we were looking for the way
up to Bernshaw Tower.

We found the lane which led to it with little trouble. However, con-
trary to what Wilkinson had indicated, the Bernshaw Tower of today is
no ruin but a sturdy farmhouse, one wing of which is in Tudor style,
with one or two of the windows long since blanked off. The farmer
agreed that this was, in fact, the Bernshaw Tower of the legend, and
it was true that a ghostly hunt was reputed to chase over these hills on
All Hallow's Eve. Despite the wintry conditions it was easy to picture
the natural speldnour of the gorge in the days before the railway and
the highway. Eagle's Crag, although out of sight at this point, would be
an easy walk along the hilltop. In an attempt to photograph the rock
however, we chose the hard way. After driving as far as possible on
bumpy snowy tracks on the hilltop, we went on foot down almost
to road-level then climbed straight up the precipitous snow-covered
wooded slopes. Once at the top it was an exhilarating experience to
stand on the jutting rock, and it was easy to picture the encounter
between the doe, the mysterious hound and the huntsman.

Almost a year passed before I was able to return to the area. On a
brilliantly clear, crisp winter's morning I stopped the car near the reser-
voirs at Dunnockshaw on the A56. With only my sketchy, hand-drawn
maps, I set off into the hills and across the rough moor of what had
been Hapton Park, to find the ruins of Hapton Tower. My information
was rudimentary.

Nearby, to the south was Tower Brook, an old quarry, and beyond,
Hameldon Hill. I had no contours to guide me and no scale of distance.
None of the features was recognisable, nor in view. Eventually however,
after plodding across country in what I assumed to be the right direction, I reached a stream. With a pair of field glasses I was able to make
out downstream what could have been an old quarry. Fortunately, it
proved to be such – no doubt the source of masonry for the tower,
whose meagre remains I found at the top of the adjacent rise. In a wall

of otherwise rough-hewn stone is a short stretch of neat rectangular blocks with small window-like openings, too small for the passage of sheep, in front of which are the cornerstones and footings of what was once a substantial building.

The site was imposing. In front the ground falls away to give a far-ranging view over the Burnley area, while behind rises Hameldon Hill, 1,300 feet high, and poised like a great wave about to break. From Hapton Tower, it must have been a three-and-a-half mile cross-country trek for Lady Sybil to reach Cliviger Mill. As the map showed, there had once been two dams, but these were now overgrown and the mill little more than a pile of nettle-covered rubble.

So ended the trail. Starting from an idea sparked off by the mural, I had been able to explore an apparently uninteresting and unfashionable part of the Yorkshire-Lancashire border to some purpose, and gain some insight into past life and thought. It seemed likely that whatever the true events were, they took place in the late 16th or early 17th century when the cult of witchcraft was at its peak.

"Lord William" remains a rather misty figure, whose name does not appear in the Towneley family archives of that period. This title might have been a cover for some other member of the family. As a character he is feeble compared with "Lady Sybil", a borderline Yorkshirewoman if ever there was one, but evidently possessing a very strong personality. One can see her independence of spirit, confined by the conventions of womanhood's role, seeking expression and fulfilment in ways which to the ordinary folk of her day were highly suspect. It is a very human situation where she becomes the submissive wife, only to tire after a year and long for her former independence. Might it not, one wonders, have been a subtle piece of Lancastrian male propaganda, designed to keep their rebellious spouses in their places? For me, and not only as a Yorkshireman, my sympathies are very strongly on the side of Lady Sybil.

Phil Levesley (1969)

BEGGAR'S BRIDGE

STANDING by the river below Glaisdale I looked at the slim, tall wisp of a bridge which is known as Beggar's Bridge and recalled the legend about it which, if not true, is certainly romantic. In the 17th century, Tom Ferris, a youth of modest means, fell in love with Squire Richardson's daughter, Agnes, who lived on the other side of the Esk, but father frowned on the affair. His daughter, he declared, would never marry a beggar, but he added the rider that if Tom ever became a man of means the matter would be reconsidered.

So Tom decided to go to foreign parts to make his fortune and arranged a final visit to his sweetheart on the eve of his departure. Alas, the river was in high flood and there was no bridge by which he could cross. The fond farewells were unspoken.

Tom went off the next day and made his fortune. He came home, married Agnes and built the bridge for the benefit of future generations. As proof of this, Tom's initials, "T.F.", and the date (1621) adorn the bridge. Tom himself later became Mayor of Hull.

(1954)

I FEEL that the true story of Thomas Ferris ought to be told. Thomas Ferris, according to Canon Atkinson, came from the upper part of Eskdale, probably Westerdale. He worked as a labourer in Egton Parish and met Agnes Richardson. Her parents were certainly not rich and whatever her father was, he was not a squire. There has never been a squire of Glaisdale, and I am fairly certain that he lived in a small cottage at Glaisdale End. A tiny bit of the cottage can be seen in the Vicarage kitchen garden.

Thomas was nearly drowned crossing the Esk and made his vow to build a bridge. Like other youths of an adventurous spirit, he went to sea and served with great courage fighting the Spanish. A Spanish ship was captured and his share of the prize set him up in business in Hull. He married Agnes, built the bridge and left great benefactions to Trinity House, Hull, to help poor mariners.

He also did not forget his wife's Parish Church for he left £6 13s. 4d. to be paid annually to the Minister of Glaisdale and £2 for the upkeep of the church. This is paid by a rent charge on a house in High Street, Hull, on St. Thomas' Day. At the time this church was a chapel-of-ease in Danby Parish.

In the '60s of last century, Glaisdale Church was re-built and altered greatly and to mark the event, Trinity House, Hull, presented to the church some very fine communion plate, two chalices, two pattens and a flagon. These are all inscribed, "presented to Glaisdale Church by the Corporation of Trinity House of Hull, in memory of Thomas Ferris, their mutual benefactor."

A board in the church records that in the will of Mr. Alderman Thomas Ferris of Hull, dated 1630, £2 a year was to be paid out of his property in High Street, Hull, to keep the church in repair.

Rev. A. Molony (1954)

BALLAD OF BEGGAR'S BRIDGE

The Dalesmen say that their light and way
Is due to an Egton man
Whose love was tried by a whelming tide
I heard the tale in his native dale
And this the Legend ran:

Why lingers my loved one; oh why does he roam
On the last winter's evening that hails him at home?
He promised to see me once more ere he went
But the long rays of gloaming all lonely I've spent.
The stones at the Fording no longer I see;
Ah, the darkness of night has concealed them from me.
The Maiden of Glazedale sat lonely at eve,
And the cold stormy night saw her hopelessly grieve.

But when she looked forth from her casement at morn
The Maiden of Glazedale was truly forlorn
For the stones were engulfed where she looked for them
By the deep swollen Esk that rolled rapidly past
And vainly she strove with her tear bedimmed eye

The pathway she gazed on last night to descry.
Her lover had come to the brink of the tide
And to stem its swift current repeatedly tried
But the rough swirling eddy still swept him ashore
And relentlessly bade him attempt it no more
Exhausted he climbed the steep side of the brae
And looked up the dale ere he turned him away
Ah, from her far window a light flickered dim
And he knew she was faithfully waiting for him.

I go to seek my fortune love
In a far far distant land,
And without thy parting blessing love
I am forced to quit the strand.
But over Arncliffe's brow my love
I see thy twinkling light,
And when deeper waters part us love
T'will be my beacon bright.
If fortune ever favours me
St. Hilda hear my vow,
No lover again in my native plain
Will be thwarted as I am now.
One day I'll come to claim my bride
As a worthy and wealthy man;
And my well-earned gold shall raise a bridge
Across this torrent's span.
The rover came back from a far distant land,
And he claimed of the maiden her long promised hand
But he built, ere he won here, the bridge of his vow
And the lovers of Egton pass over it now.

S.A. Jackson (1959)

TALES FROM OLD WHITBY

WHITBY is rich in the lore of the Abbess Hilda, the first Abbess to
follow the foundation of the Abbey by Oswy, King of Northumbria.
That was about the year 656, and by the time of her death in 680 Hilda
had secured for the Abbey a high place among the religious centres of
the country.

Hilda's work in north-east Yorkshire was so distinctive that it survives the years not only in local history but in legend. Sea-birds flying over the Abbey were reputed to lower their wings and sink to the ground in homage, and the famous fossil beds round the town have been accounted by non-scientific people as dating from the time when Hilda relieved the district of a plague of snakes by praying off the heads and then praying them into stone.

How many young men make the pilgrimage to "Black Nab" on Hallowe'en in these times? One of Whitby's most colourful legends tells that a pirate crew stole the bells of the Abbey. They put to sea again but did not get very far. Their vessel foundered on the ridge of "Black Nab" and cargo and crew were lost. Out of the incident arose a local custom whereby if a young man loved a girl and visited "Black Nab" on Hallowe'en, calling out her name, his voice would re-echo on the breeze and in the background he would hear prophetic marriage chimes from the bells the pirates stole and lost.

John Priestley (1950)

TREASURE TROVE!

SIR Thomas Slingsby, Lord of the Manor of Knaresborough in 1805, usually disliked interruptions to his meals, but the information that one of his estate workers had something of interest to show the squire,

intrigued him greatly. A few moments later and the man, cap in hand, stood before him, while on the Sheraton table lay a worn leather bag. Excitedly, Sir Thomas pulled open the strings and a shower of silver coins, 600 in all, spilled on to the polished surface; coins of the reign of Edward I and obviously, he calculated, from the description of their place of concealment, a hoard, hidden from the ravaging Scots after the English defeat at Bannockburn in 1314. The man, to give Sir Thomas his due, was awarded the full intrinsic value of the find and was amply satisfied.

During the 1950s especially, developments on a large scale uncovered a number of interesting finds, comprising not only gold sovereigns, but also long out-dated bank notes and bringing to the mind the ever-romantic vision of treasure. Of all the words in the English language this must rank high with its ability to fire the imagination, but a treasure may be an antique, or an hierloom, or simply a "treasured" item, worth-less intrinsically, but of immeasurable sentimental value; most of us possess something of the sort. Bullion, however, is another matter. Its origins are often violent historically, comprised of the plunder of war and destruction.

Once known as Darien, the "Golden Isthmus" of Panama is steeped in tales of filibusters and buccaneers and to gaze upon one of the most glorious of its remaining treasures, "The Golden Altar of San Jose", in its beautiful old Spanish church in Panama City, is a thrill indeed. By it being white-washed to assimilate plaster, this work of art escaped the terrible Sack of Panama by the Welsh-born pirate Sir Henry Morgan, in 1671 – "a glory lost forever" says a plaque on the old ruined walls. Old Panama's great Cathedral once rivalled that of Cuzco, in the New World, and its great bell could be heard across trackless miles of jungle and fever-swamp.

From a glory built upon the murder of an Inca King and an Aztec Emperor and the ensalvement of their peoples, Old Panama fell to an even more ruthless hand and now pelicans wheel overhead like sparrows; long green lizards seek the shelter of its crumbling stones against he tropic sun, while at Balboa on the Pacific Coast, rusted iron rings embedded in a sea-worn stone are pointed to tourists as the place where screaming prisoners were tied to feed the sharks in the days of Spanish tyranny.

Yorkshire cannot rival the splendour of the Mildenhall (Suffolk) treasure, or the fascination of the Tobermory Galleon on the Isle of Mull, but Kirkstall Abbey has the legend of a treasure which escaped the hands of Thomas Cromwell's Commissioners at the Dissolution. Dob (once Dog) Park Castle, a former hunting lodge of the great Vavasour family, is said to have given up its rich secret to the laid of the Vavasours about 1810, while Weston Hall, near Otley, home of the Dawsons, who are descended from the Vavasours, is said to have a treasure guarded by the spectre of a great black dog.

Yet another legend speaks of Knaresborough Castle, which once had a long-vanished donkey-skin chart, or map, showing the whereabouts of a long-lost well in which was hidden the pre-Civil War Crown of England. With the movement of armies during the Civil War (1642-49), families of both persuasions hastily concealed their valuables on the approach of the enemy. Hollow beams, loose stones and chimney flues are still revealing their time-worn secrets with patient investigation and more ruthless demolition.

In 1833, workmen removing soil in Pudsey uncovered a cache of silver coins of the reigns of Elizabeth, James I and Charles I, excelling in value even the hoard of silver coins of pre-Julius Caesar date found in a cave on Pudsey Common in 1775. Another Civil War find came to light at Garforth, near Leeds, in 1826, when workmen, on removing an ancient wall, found a leather purse containing 41 pieces of coin of Elizabeth, James I and Charles I vintage. Tudor and Stuart coins were

also found in 1924, at Scholes, but one of the most rewarding finds
came in 1837, in the more romantic setting of Victoria Cave, Settle.

In that year a Mr. Joseph Jackson took his dog for a walk along the
limestone escarpment. Chasing a rabbit, the animal disappeared through
a small opening in the rock and he called its name; its answering bark
produced a hollow sound, indicating a large space inside. By lying full
length on his stomach, Mr. Jackson managed to enter by clawing away
at nettles and the obstruction of years, and later (rather oddly) spent

whole nights exploring the cave. He found many relics of earlier occupation such as implements of bone and bronze and also a large quantity
of copper and silver coins of the three Roman Constantine emperors.

Another interesting hoard is said to be buried deep in Ivescar Caves,
also known as Boggart Holes, at Ivescar House. It is an exceedingly
dangerous cave to enter in bad weather; flood waters have washed into
the light of day silver coins of the reign of Edward I, believed to be part
of a large treasure concealed by local people in the war-torn days of the
Scottish raids which harassed the north in the 14th century. Gold coins
of a later period have also been found and local tradition has it that
"loads of gold" still lie hidden waiting for the lucky finder, although
numerous attempts have been made to penetrate this "Aladdin's Cave"
of the Dales.

About 1720, a copper urn, holding a Treasure Trove of 600 silver
denarii of the Roman emperors Alexander Severus and Gordianus
Pius (A.D. 222-244), was found at a spot roughly half-way between

Ribchester and Overborough, probably hidden because of the general unrest in the Empire at that period. At Overborough, once a Roman Station like Settle, a certain Miss Fenwick discovered in the early 19th century a valuable *aurea bulla*, a hollow ball of pure gold, said to be the only object of its kind in Britain. These insignia were heart-shaped and worn round the necks of Roman soldiers for valour in battle.

Large hoards of lesser intrinsic, but not necessarily archaeological or historical value have been found, such as the large cache uncovered in one of the ancient quarries at Castleberg, Settle, in 1783. These coins were mostly of the much-minted Constantine period and mostly of copper or bronze. It was two successful, though not valuable, finds during the Dig for Victory Campaign in 1944, at Farsley, that encouraged my own interest in buried money, but regrettably attempts at panning for gold in the Baw Baw Ranges of Victoria, Australia in 1959, produced no suddenly acquired wealth; the goal of all treasure-hunters.

So much more speculation could be written about the possibility of uncovering further hoards in Yorkshire alone, but regrettably, we can only add one last word to this fascinating subject. This must be given to certainly one of the county's most colourful, romantic and greatest discoveries, namely the golden ring of Aethelswith, Queen of Mercia. This beautiful piece of jewellery was ploughed up in a field between Aberford and Sherburn, in 1870. Thinking the article pretty, but value-less, the farmer attached it to the collar of his dog as an ornament or charm.

Chatting one day with a more educated man, the stranger noticed the dog's collar-souvenir and eventually it was through his efforts that it was identified as a ring which once adorned the finger of a Saxon princess, a royal lady of Yorkshire's Dark Ages. It is now one of the nation's most treasured possessions. Take a tip from me; before throwing that stone or pebble for your dog when next you take a country walk; have another look at it before you let go. It may be treasure.

Donald Wagstaff (1969)

A FAIRY BANQUET

TWO tumuli mark the eastern and western end of what is known as "The Great Wold Valley". The western tumuli can be seen at the road-side at Duggleby, a small village about six miles north of Driffield. The eastern end, where one sees the Willy Howe, is nearer Bridlington, on the left, at a sharp corner near Wold Newton.

Howe is the Scandinavian word for small round hill, and that is what these tumuli are. Under them the old chieftains were buried, along with their followers and those possessions thought to be necessary for existence in the next world.

There are many such tumuli on the Wolds, not raised in a haphazard manner but suggesting a certain amount of religious thought. It has been realised that they were planned after the shape of the constellation of the Great Bear, and in the case of the Willy Howe a legend grew about it. It tells of a young man who was returning to his home at Wold Newton late at night. As he passed the Willy Howe he heard sounds of revelry.

Tying his horse to a tree, he ventured up the farm track and was amazed to see that a great door was open in the side of the Willy Howe; he peered into this doorway and saw fairies holding a banquet. Lights sparkled, music was heard and the table was laid with delicacies, wine being served from golden goblets.

The fairies became aware of his presence and one of them, coming to the doorway, offered him wine from one of the golden goblets. About to drink, the young man paused, for he remembered that to drink fairy wine is to give up human shape and become one of the fairies.

Dashing the goblet to the ground he turned about and ran for his horse with the infuriated fairies in hot pursuit. Yelling with rage they followed him as he made for home but coming to the stream that was called the Vipse he remembered that fairy folk will not cross flowing water. The Vipse was in full spate. He set his horse for the water and was safe.

Nowadays the Vipse is known as the Gypsey Race. It is said to rise at Wharram-le-Street, but the little stream there is constantly flowing and the Gypsey Race flows sometimes. So one looks for it near Wold Newton where, when it does flow, it runs on to Burton Fleming, Rudstone and into the harbour at Bridlington.

It is a mystery stream, supposed to emerge in times of disaster, and when it began to flow in the olden days, the maidens from the nearby villages threw flowers upon the water to placate the gods.

Such streams are due to an accumulation of water among the chalk layers underground. One would think that constant wet weather would set the stream flowing, but the Gypsey Race emerges in times of drought, which has puzzled folk right down the ages. Almost supernatural powers have been attributed to the stream.

Florence Hopper (1972)

THERE'S ROMANCE AT THE BOTTOM OF A WELL

THE frequency of "well" in Yorkshire place names is an indication of the importance attached to springs and wells dating back to those Norse and Danish times when names and places became associated. Although Yorkshire has never adopted the ceremony of well dressing, as performed in Derbyshire, or the "blessing of the waters", performed elsewhere, it has always taken a poetical as well as a practical interest in its water supply, and this applies to all three Ridings. Each Riding has its plentiful supply of springs and wells to which attach legends and traditions. Each has its natural oddities of water supply.

Just outside Settle, in the West Riding, on the main road to Kendal and at the foot of the limestone cliff of Giggleswick Scar, is the Ebbing and Flowing Well which proved so great a puzzle to early scientists and a poetic theme for most literary travellers. The well itself is an insignificant stone basin in which the water periodically ebbs and flows, sometimes rising several inches in the hour, sometimes almost stationary. On rare occasions, although not in recent years, a line of bubbles like a silver cord has been seen in the well and has conferred a great novelty upon it.

Michael Drayton, in his *Polyolbion*, written 350 years ago, conferred upon the well the legend of a nymph pursued by a Satyr and turned into a spring to avoid the clutch of her pursuer. The poet saw in the ebb and flow of the water the quick gasps for breath of the pursued nymph, a poetic fantasy which the modern age discounts in favour of a more scientific theory of a syphon in the rocks behind the well. In more recent times the well became the frequent resort of Settle children, who made from the water and lumps of liquorice Spanish Wine, as they termed it, of high colour but no potency.

In the East Riding is the Drummer Boy's Well of Harpham. From a casual glance it might be a field pond, but it shares two traditions which have given it fame. The first declares that when William the Conqueror took part in a battle near the village of Harpham, he promised to give the village, and the land about it, to the first man who would set foot within it. A drummer boy was the first to reach the village and could have claimed the reward, but a knight named St. Quintin who followed close behind him, seeing the prize vanish from his grasp, knocked the drummer boy into a nearby well and claimed the Conqueror's reward. Hence the name of the well, and hence, too, the legend that the sound of the beating of a drum can be heard at the bottom of the well whenever the head of the house of St. Quintin is to die.

The other legend dates from the time of Edward II, when the youth of the village were training in archery, and the competitions took place in the pasture near the well. Once more a St. Quintin figures in the story, for the squire of that name had a hired boy, Tom, the son of Molly Hewson, reputed to be the wise woman of Harpham. Tom was the drummer of the local band of archers, and on the day of the competition led the archers on to the field.

When the display took place, one youth among them proved clumsy with his bow, and the angry squire, whip in hand, strode forward to beat him. But in his anger he bumped against the drummer Tom, who was hurled into the well, where he died. Molly Hewson, frantic with grief, addressed the squire and warned him that whenever a St. Quintin was about to die, the spirit of the boy would go back into the well and beat his drum. Thus it became a doom well.

Near the road from Richmond to Askrigg is the North Riding's most noteworthy spring, the Hart Leap Well. In itself insignificant, it has achieved immortality from Wordsworth's poem describing the manner in which it received its name. According to the poet it happened that one day long ago a gay company of knights and ladies from Wensleydale were out in pursuit of deer, and they followed a noble hart up the dale for hour after hour. But as the chase, and the day, went on, the hunters began to tire and drop out of the chase, until a solitary knight and his dogs were left to pursue the weary beast. And even the dogs tired and fell gasping among the mountain fern.

Where is the throng, the tumult of the race?
The bugles that so joyfully were blown?
This chase it looks not like an earthly chase;
Sir Walter and the hart are left alone.

The poor hart toils along the mountainside;
I will not stop to tell how far he fled,
Nor will I mention by what death he died;
But now the knight beholds him lying dead.

The body of the hart was lying close to a tiny spring, the waters of which were still disturbed by its dying breath, but Sir Walter was less affected by the death of the animal – which in fact appeared to please him – than by the fact that he found three hoof-marks, indicating that the beast had taken a mighty leap from the hill-top to the fountain.

Sir Walter wiped his face, and cried, "Till now
Such sight was never seen by living eyes;
Three leaps have borne him from this lofty brow
Down to the very fountain where he lies.

"I'll build a pleasure-house upon this spot,
And a small arbour make for rural joy;
'Twill be the traveller's shed, the pilgrim's cot,
A place of love for damsels that are coy.

"A cunning artist will I have to frame
A basin for that fountain in the dell!
And they who do make mention of the same,
From this day forth, shall call it Hart Leap Well."

In a second part to the poem, Wordsworth laments that the arbour – which by now had become a mansion – had all vanished in the course of time, and only the fountain and a shepherd's legend were left to mark the place.

These three notable wells symbolise the high regard Yorkshire people have always had for the sources of water, and a determination to find romance at the bottom of a well. Such romance became enshrined in legend, and that fact conferred upon the wells as added prestige and gave to their waters a deeper significance.

There are wells in the Craven district dedicated to the Empress Helen or Helena, the Blessed Virgin, St. Margaret, and other deities, which at one time had special virtues attached to them, and were held in great reverence and veneration. The Empress Helen was the wife of the Roman Emperor Constantius, who died at York in 306, and the mother of Constantine the Great, the succeeding Emperor. Both the Empress and her son were noble champions of Christianity, and she is credited with being the discoverer of the true cross. Wells dedicated to St. Helen exist, or did exist, at Burnsall and Denton, in Wharfedale, and Eshton and Farnhill, in Airedale.

A well at Burnsall was also dedicated to St. Margaret, but evidently there is some doubt as to who this St. Margaret really was. One writer tells us that the spring was dedicated to St. Margaret of Antioch, "a virgin martyr, whose fame surpassed nearly every other in England in the thirteenth century." Another states that this well was dedicated "to that pure and noble Saxon lady, Margaret, wife of Malcom Canmore, King of Scotland, who was born in 1046, and during her lifetime endowed many religious houses."

The existence of a well near the Embsay Vicarage, known as Nun's Well, has led more than one writer to wonder if a nunnery at one time existed in the vicinity, but there is nothing to indicate this; not even tradition. St. Helen's Well, at Eshton, is stated to have petrifying properties, and takes its name from an old endowed chapel-of-ease dedicated to this early Christian saint. There are no remains of this church to be seen today, but it is mentioned in a commission relating to the Manor of

Flasby in 1429, and field adjoining the site is known as Chapel Field, while "Saint Helen Lands" are mentioned in old documents.

Kettlewell derives its name from the owner of a well, "Ketel's Well", and a well in Grasswood, near Grassington, is given the name of "Beggar's Gill Well".

Legends, traditions and stories are associated with all these wells; one at Threshfield, dedicated to the Blessed Virgin, being "a safe refuge from all supernatural visitants, hob-goblins and the like". Old Pam was a famous Threshfield goblin, and one night, while Pam and his imps were making merry in the Threshfield school, dancing to the tune of a fiddle, Dan Cooper, a noted local character, on his way home from the village ale house, heard these sounds of revelry and peeped in. Unfortunately, he betrayed his presence with a sneeze and had to run for his life. He took sanctuary in "Our Lady's Well", and though the imps dare not molest him there, they kept Dan up to the neck in icy cold water until the crowing of a cock announced the approach of dawn and the time for their departure.

It is an old custom in Yorkshire to wish at wells. And young ladies who wished to see their lovers mirrored in the waters would visit a well secretly and drop a pin, usually bent, or on some occasions a silver coin, if possible a crooked one, into the spring. Occasionally, it is said, love-lorn bachelors would perform the same ceremony, but whether successfully or not is rarely revealed. A port described the custom when he wrote:

She had dreamt as she lay in her lonely cote
That the fairies would be kind,
And for one bright pin or a shilling groat
Dropt into the well, if it did not float;
In its place she would surely find
The sweet vision of him whom her heart most craves,
Rise clear to her view on the rippling waves.

Similar to the pin wells were the rag wells, where it was believed ailments could be cured or wishes realised by the spirit of the well. The person who wished to benefit had to arrive before sunrise, face a tree near the water, take some portion of a garment from his or her person, dip it into the water, tie a knot in it, and then place it on the tree that was faced, expressing the wish meanwhile for the object needed. Until comparatively recently it was not uncommon for trees near wells to be found decorated with the rags of old garments and remnants of new. Yet despite the efficacy of the well to conjure up the portraits of lovers or to cure ailments, there is little evidence that Yorkshire folk ever regarded wells as haunted or treated them with any fear. Apparently water was regarded as a practical agency rather than a supernatural one.

The only exception to this general rule is that associated with the Gypsey Race in the East Riding. The race of a stream, fed by several erratic springs near Wharram-le-Street. The stream runs for some miles through Lutton and Weaverthorpe and then vanishes underground to appear again near Wold Newton, as several springs. These once more re-form to make a new race, which flows through Burton Fleming to Rudston and enters the sea at Bridlington, near the Quay, a total journey of some twenty miles.

The rising of the waters that make the race was long regarded with reverence, and the appearance of the waters was always treated as a portent of war, famine or other evils. Tradition asserts that the race ran strongly before the Great Plague of 1665, before the Restoration of Charles II, before the fall of a great meteor at Wold Newton, and before several great floods, which devastated the district. Rather oddly, too, the Waters of Woe were in full spate just before the outbreak of the First World War and not long before the second.

(1958)

DID THE REAL ROBIN HOOD LIVE IN BARNSDALE?

WHETHER or not Robin Hood was a real-life person has not been definitely proved. He may have been a hero devised with several bowmen-outlaws, living in adjacent areas, in mind. He has come to represent the individual's fight for freedom against tyranny, corrupt officialdom and selfish interests that ignored the rights of the common man.

The theme was romanticised in larer years. Most of the illusions that we hold about the idyllic life that Robin and his Merry Men led in the greenwood stem from the amazing output of Victorian writers and illustrators. In the Victorian and Edwardian periods, archery became popular with both men and women.

Much of the material about Robin Hood's adventures was written after his supposed existence; it was handed down and embroidered by travelling minstrels in the form of ballads and songs. These stories were written down and eventually printed. The best know, *The Lytell Geste of Robyn Hode*, is much quoted and used in later stories about the outlaw and his men.

In these rhymes, direct reference is made to Barnsdale, in Yorkshire, as the area in which Robin Hood had his headquarters – i.e. at "a grene-wode tre".

> *Robin strode in Bernesdale,*
> *And lenyd hym to a tre;*
> *And bi hym stode Litell Johnn,*
> *A guide yeman was he.*

Nowhere does the *Geste* refer to Sherwood Forest, though Nottingham is mentioned. Barnsdale can be firmly identified as being in the Doncaster district and the story of Little John's encounter with the potter at "Wentbreg" can only be Wentbridge, 10 miles north of Doncaster and at the northern limits of the old Barnsdale Forest. Little John was quoted as being very familiar with Barnsdale's "gates" and "knows each one".

Legend has it that Robin went to Nottingham to take part in an archery contest there. He went in disguise, his face hidden by his raised hood. Maybe his surname "Hood" was a nickname to conceal his real identity. Certainly someone with a reputation as a great bowman lived in the forest and over the centuries his name has become synonymous with the common man's stand against tyranny. Another place name mentioned in the *Geste* is "Saylis":

> *And walke up to the Saylis,*
> *And so to Watlinge Street,*
> *And wayte after some unketh gest,*
> *Up chance ye may them mete.*

These are the instructions Robin have to Little John with regard to apprehending a victim. The Saylis is now preserved as "Sayle's Plantation", at the northernmost edge of Barnsdale and 500 yards east of Wentbridge. As early as the 13th century, the road which runs north-west from Barnsdale was called "Watlinge Street".

Various places are associated with characters who lived in the "greenwood". In Taxal Churchyard, Cheshire, is a large yew tree from which it is said the bows were made for Robin Hood and his men. In Hathersage churchyard, a large thigh-bone was unearthed which is said to have been the thigh-bone of John Littel (Little John), who was a Derbyshire man.

In the Middle Ages the woods spread right across the counties of Nottinghamshire, Yorkshire, and parts of Cheshire and Derbyshire so maybe the outlaws moved around a lot to avoid detection. Some sources indicate that Robin Hood was only an outlaw in the greenwood for about 18 months, so it is hard to understand why, as an old man, about 22 years later, he still had a "price on his head" when he visited his cousin, the prioress at Kirklees, near Brighouse, to ask for medication and bleeding.

It was said that the Prioress bled him too much, to cause his death and share the proceeds with her lover, Sir Roger, of "Donkestere"

(Doncaster), but Robin had his faithful friend, Little John, with him and John helped to pull his bow and fire his last arrow. The point the arrow landed on was to be his burial place:

> *And where the arrow is taken up,*
> *There shall my grave diggd be.*
> *With verdant sod most neatly put,*
> *Sweet as the green wood tree.*

> *And lay my bent bow by my side,*
> *Which was my music sweet,*
> *And make my grave of gravel and green,*
> *Which is most right and meet.*

After the novels and plays about Robin Hood came the film and T.V. versions of the story. The best film on the subject is surely *The Adventures of Robin Hood* filmed in "glorious Technicolour" by First National. The only criticism I have is that hills are shown in the distance were the pointed hills of California!

J.W. Marsland (1986)

ROBIN OF BARNSDALE

MISCONCEPTIONS about the situation of Sherwood Forest and the area of authority of the Sheriff of Nottingham have given rise to the belief that Robin was a man of the Midlands. This is against all the evidence which shows Robin Hood to have been born in Yorkshire; here he spent most of his life. Here, too, he died.

The ballads provide most of our detailed knowledge of Robin Hood. These tales were a most popular form of mediaeval entertainment. Poetic licence was permissible; the writer could whitewash and glamorise his hero, but the basis of the story must be true else the ballad had little chance of success and none of survival.

Ballads recounting the deeds of Robin Hood and his companions are of very early date. Despite later romances which assign their activities to the reigns of Richard I and Prince John their true period appears to be the mid-14th century during the reigns of Edwards II and III. The most famous complete ballad *The Lyttel Geste* was published in 1489, although it was written much earlier and was compiled from still earlier ballads no doubt familiar to many who had actually met and known Robin Hood.

According to these ballads Robin Hood was born in Wakefield the son

of a forester. They give no clue as to how or why he became an outlaw but having achieved that unenviable state we are informed that he centred himself in Barnsdale. Barnsdale was a tract of forest in the south part of the West Riding bounded in the north by the River Went and extending between Askern and Badsworth.

It was a popular haunt of brigands. Travellers of importance normally heavily guarded always increased their escort before crossing this part of Sherwood. The forest was, of course, part of the greater forest of Sherwood, which extended as its name implies across the borders of the three counries of York, Derby and Nottingham.

It was in Barnsdale that, according to the ballads, Robin Hood met King Edward III who granted a pardon to the outlaw, took him off to court and rewarded him with some sort of minor post. But this break with the greenwood was short lived. Hood was back in Barnsdale within a few months and lived out the remainder of his life once again outside the law until finally he died, at the hands of his kinswoman, the Prioress of Kirklees, near Brighouse.

This is the story from the ballads and, to the discomfort of the critics, it is remarkable how well it is confirmed by contemporary records of unquestionable authenticity. A century ago the Reverend Joseph Hunter began a long research into the life and times of Robin Hood and more lately Dr. J.W. Walker, who conducted a research into the Wakefield Manorial Court Rolls, has produced more evidence which appears to uphold the traditional story.

The ballad begins "The father of Robin a forester was…" There are many references in the Court Rolls to an Adam Hood who frequently appeared in court as a surety in the early 14th century. Some time later a Robert (Robin) Hood is mentioned together with his wife Matilda (Marion). They evidently had a reasonable station in life and the Rolls record the sale of a plot of land in Wakefield to the couple where they subsequently built a house.

With such a promising start in life – a respectable father, a new wife and property – one would hardly expect the young Robin ever to become an outcast from society. Official records, however, confirm that the house of Robert and Matilda Hood was forfeited to the crown and we can assume that Robin Hood was outlawed sometime in the reign of Edward II.

The fact that the ballads give no reason for Robin's disgrace leads one to suppose that his crime must have been something uncomplimentary; something that the ballad writers preferred not to mention. It could not have been merely an infringement of the forest laws but was probably, as some writers have suggested, the serious crime of treason.

Wakefield at this time was in the Lordship of the Earl of Lancaster. When this gentleman rebelled against the unpopular Edward II many Wakefield men followed him to the disastrous Battle of Boroughbridge. It was a Royal victory culminating in the execution of Lancaster and the leading rebels but many of the rank and file escaped the king's vengeance by taking to the woods. It is probable that Robin Hood was one of this number and the nucleus of his band of Merry Men were most certainly fellow fugitives from justice.

Some of the outlaw band are named in the ballads. There was Much the son of the Miller of Wakefield, Will Scathlock (Scarlet) and Little John who was to become almost as famous as Robin Hood himself. No mention is made in the early ballads of Maid Marion but she may have existed as Mistress Matilda. Friar Tuck, too, appears to be a much later invention and must be regarded as a fiction. On the other hand it is possible to accept Tuck as a generic term for the number of friars who, in all probability, ministered to the outcasts of the woods.

In spite of his banditry Robin Hood is shown in most of the records as a religious man. The *Scotichronicon*, a 14th century document, states that the outlaw refused to interrupt his attendance at Mass even when the Sheriff and his men were at hand and other records attribute the building of an oratory in Barnsdale to Robin Hood. Someone, therefore, must have brought the consolations of the Church to the outlaws, and who else but the friars? These were mendicant priests unattached to parishes and their grey habits would probably be familiar to the unfortunates of the woods.

Since most of Robin Hood's adult life was lived in outlawry he was hunted not by one but by many Sheriffs of Nottingham as well as other law officers. By the law of averages it was inevitable that the law would triumph in the end.

The ballads imply that Robin created the law and died at the hands of his kinswoman, the prioress of Kirklees, to whom he had turned for aid in his sickness. Reading between the lines, however, it was not a sick man who turned up at Brighouse and Kirklees but a wounded man. The king had begun an intensive drive against outlaws and the truth of the matter is that Robin and his men had been outfought by the king's men.

It is a pity that the ballads are not explicit here but it is understandable. They are glossing over unpalatable facts to provide the hero with an acceptable death.

The poor prioress of Kirklees has been made the villain of the piece but it is doubtful whether any motive could be found to explain why a dedicated woman should harm anyone, least of all her kinsman. Let us not dispute the story that Robin died as she bled him. She was merely following the accepted medical practice of the day and if he had already lost blood through wounds the extra loss by "blood-letting" would, no doubt, accelerate his end. He was buried in the grounds of Kirklees Priory and the prioress has been slandered ever since.

So ended the career of Robin Hood, a Yorkshire bandit famed throughout the English-speaking world. He has another claim to fame that has been overlooked. In the Wakefield Court Rolls under the date 1st May, 1309, is an entry of a fine of twopence on a Robert Hode for stealing firewood. Perhaps this also establishes our outlaw as our most notorious juvenile delinquent.

J.A. Clough (1965)

THE MOST FAMOUS BOWMAN OF THEM ALL

NO account of archery in Yorkshire would be complete without mention of Robin Hood, the most famous bowman of them all. Whether he was one man or several, real life or legend, it is reasonable to situate him on the south-eastern border of the county, where he could shuttle conveniently between Nottinghamshire's Sherwood Forest and Yorkshire's Forest of Barnsdale, in the Barnsley-Rotherham-Sheffield-Doncaster area.

The traveller up the A1 encounters, almost as soon as he enters the county, at the northern end of the Doncaster by-pass, Robin Hood's Well by the roadside; and from them on Yorkshire contains many references to his presence and his exploits, some thirty in all, natural and archeological features, right up to Robin Hood's Bay, where he shot an arrow from one headland to the other.

He visited Fountains Abbey, stung by a taint of Will Scarlett's that:

The curtal Fryer in Fountain-Abby
Well can draw a good strong bow.
He will beat both you and your yeoman,
Set them all in a row.

The encounter resulted in a ducking in the river Skell for Robin and for Friar Tuck ("curtal" because he wore a short or curtailed gown) and a permanent friendship. Robin Hood's Wood and another Robin Hood's Well are still features of the Fountain's estate.

In the end, Robin, a sick man, was placed in the care of the Prioress of Kirklees, near Huddersfield, who for reasons of her own bled him to death. A bowman to the last breath, he shot one final and famous arrow from his death-bed with the injunction that he be buried where the arrow struck. His wish was carried out his tomb may still be seen there.

Whatever celestial butts he may now be gracing, the bowmen of Yorkshire salute him, and they can assure him that the practice of archery still flourishes in Yorkshire, with the good company and good fellowship which have always accompanied it.

Howard Strick (1977)

Part 5

Tales from the Towns

ROYAL CAPTURE

THE street name, King Charles' Croft, in the centre of Leeds was for a long time a reminder that nearby stood Red House where that king was once held as a prisoner – and refused a chance to escape. Ralph Thoresby, the historian of Leeds, tells the story, though how much is history and how much is legend in uncertain. Here is his account:

"When Charles I was being conveyed a prisoner to London by his gaoler, Cornet Joyce, he was lodged in the Red House here. A maid-servant of the house entreated him to put on her clothes and make his escape, assuring him that she would conduct him in the dark out of the garden door into a back alley called Land's Lane, and thence to a friend's house from which he might make his escape to France. The King however, declined the woman's offer with many thanks, and gave her a token so that on the sight of that token his son would reward her. After the Restoration the woman presented the token to the King, and told him the story. The King enquired whence she came; she said, 'From Leeds in Yorkshire'; whether she had a husband; she replied, 'Yes'; what was his calling?; she said, 'An under-bailiff'. 'Then,' said the King, 'he shall be chief bailiff in Yorkshire.'"

THE GREAT BOFFIN HOAX

HOW many of the older generation of Leeds people remember the great Boffin hoax which began in Leeds? Old Liberals ought certainly to recall it, for it was a great mystery in the party. It may still be a mystery to some.

It arose from an article which the late Augustine Birrell wrote in a weekly paper in which, wishing to illustrate an argument, he used the name of a purely fictitious character, Tobias Boffin. Immediately there came a letter from a very angry correspondent of that name purporting to be a Unitarian minister but actually non-existent except in the minds of certain humorist friends of Mr. Birrell's who created him to puzzle the writer.

It happened that a meeting of the National Liberal Federation was about to be held in Leeds, so Sir Robert Hudson, who was in the conspiracy and was an important Liberal official, had the name of the "Rev. Tobias Boffin" inserted in the conference papers next to that of Herbert Samuel as being among those attending. The name actually appeared in a number of newspaper accounts. To carry the joke still further, a letter appeared in the *Liberal Magazine* from the same fictitious worthy objecting to the use of his name by Mr. Birrell, and the plotters even went so far as to announce in *The Times* a marriage by "the Rev. Tobias Boffin, B.A., father of the bride."

Mr. Birrell and other Liberals were greatly perturbed by the matter and it is said that, although Mr. Birrell at times suspected a hoax, he also consulted several University lists to find the name of Boffin among the B.A.s. His confusion was increased when, on one occasion, a card was sent up to him in the House by "Mr. Boffin", asking for an interview. When he went to the Lobby he was told that the reverend gentleman "had just left".

Later a "Boffin Book" was published telling the whole story of the hoax and illustrated with sketches of Boffin at the ages of seven, 37, and "present day". But there may still be some who believe the Rev. Tobias Boffin, B.A., to be a real person.

WHAT'S IN A NAME?

THERE is a curious link between the Clapham family of North Craven and Potternewton Park in Leeds, if a recent legend is to be believed. The story goes that one day a century or so ago a Mr. Thomas Clapham, who resided at the mansion of Potternewton, was called on by a solicitor who had journeyed from Settle to Leeds to inform him he had been left an estate worth between £4,000 and £5,000 a year (very considerable for those days). The benefactor was Thomas Clapham, of whom the Leeds man had never heard and whom he had never seen.

Suspecting a bad joke, the legatee made inquiries and found that the will and bequest were both in order if eccentric. Apparently the benefactor had, a long time before, seen a carriage and pair at some public function. He enquired whose it was and was told that by coincidence it belonged to a Mr. Thomas Clapham. This tickled his sense of humour and he promptly decided to make out his will in favour of the unknown namesake. "Won't the old devil stare when he gets it?" he muttered with glee as he signed the document.

FIRE!

MANY good stories are told in Yorkshire about its fire brigades in the days when these were purely local institutions. They are legendary of course, like many stories about well-loved things, and they are mainly concerned with the discomfiture of the brigade. For example, the story of the great inspection and march-past of the Brighouse Fire Brigade which took place a generation or two ago. The whole force turned out and was inspected by its chief, resplendent in a pair of white gloves. He then roared out the order to form fours. There was a shuffling in the ranks, and one of the brigade ventured a protest. "Nay George," he said, "tha' knows there's nobbut three of us without thee."

"All right, then," said the Superintendent of the Brighouse Fire Brigade sadly, "fall in, two deep."

There is the equally legendary story of how the old Thorne horse-drawn fire brigade (now equipped with a smart motor engine) was once called out, and after waiting an hour for the horse to turn up, they decided to push the engine to the fire themselves. When they got there they found that the Doncaster Fire Brigade had put the fire out and gone home.

PONTEFRACT CAKES

LIQUORICE root, so long associated with Pontefract, has a remarkable history, part fact and part legend. Ancient peoples must have known the root as a medicine for it is mentioned on the clay tablets of Babylon and recorded by the early Egyptians, Greeks and Romans. It was imported into this country for the same purpose in the 16th century, but many folk have wondered how it became a confection.

The story goes that a certain worthy schoolmaster of Pontefract was on holiday at the coast at the time of the Spanish Armada. Wandering along the beach one day he picked up a bundle of twigs washed ashore from a wrecked galleon, and it occurred to him that they would serve the purpose and save the expense of birch-twigs as a means of inflicting punishment. He soon had occasion to try them out on his return to Pontefract and so effective was his new "cane" that his boys were driven to pick up shreds from his twigs and stuff them in their mouths to stifle their cries. They discovered that the sweet flavour not only offset the pain but was something new in the way of sweetmeats when these were few in the land.

Beatings became highly popular and the liquorice twigs were soon worn out, but fragments which had been swept out of the school into the garden took root and flourished exceedingly in the soil of Pontefract. Soon the liquorice crop became a local industry with a bye-law to forbid growers to sell or give away roots. "Pontefract cakes" acquired a world-wide fame but the only link with the schoolmaster's find was in the by-name of "Spanish" which Yorkshire children often called the long strips of black liquorice.

SHEPHERD LORD

IN the peaceful courtyard of the old castle of Skipton, when the stones reflect the colour of the sky and the venerable yew tree in the centre gives a warmth and a sense of life to this historic place, legend and reality merge. Was the story of the "Shepherd Kird" fact or fiction?

It was in one of those long, low rooms overlooking the courtyard that the proud and handsome Lady Clifford sat with her three children, and attendants busy with distaff and spinning wheel, on a spring evening in 1461. Not many days before, on Palm Sunday, the fearful battle of Towton between the House of York and Lancaster had been fought, but as yet no news had reached the castle. Lord Clifford, as a supporter of the King, Henry VI, and Queen Margaret, had placed his forces at the disposal of the Red Rose against the rebel Yorkists, and they had been to the forefront at Towton. There were many anxious hearts that night among the homesteads of Craven, and not the least of these was Lady Clifford's. As the little company sat and spun and waited, a trumpet sounded and a few moments later a knight who gave the name of Sir

John de Barnoldswick, was admitted and made obeisance. "Whence comest thou and with what tidings, Sir Knight?" asked Lady Clifford anxiously.

"I come from the field of battle, lady, and my tidings are evil," was the reply. Only after much questioning and with great hesitation did the worthy knight disclose that the Lancastrian cause had lost at Towton field, that the King and Queen had fled, and that Lord Clifford was dead from an arrow wound in the throat. Despite the hesitation of the knight, the shock was very great for Lady Clifford. She cared less for herself than for her children and home, for in those days the death of a great Lord was often followed by the extermination of his family and the sequestration of their estates. And Lord Clifford was not loved by the Yorkists. Her fears were not unnecessary; as soon as the new King Edward of York was on the throne orders went forth for the handing over of Skipton Castle and the estates of Lord Clifford to supporters of the new King, and rumours came that the children were to be placed in captivity.

Disguised as a farmer's wife, Lady Clifford set out with one or two attendants and the children to her father's estate at Londesborough near Market Weighton, passing through Otley, Tadcaster and York, but keeping as much as possible to the by-roads. They arrived safely and there remained some time until news came that the Yorkists, having discovered that Skipton Castle was empty, had determined to find the young Cliffords and that Londesborough was suspected. Once more Lady Clifford was compelled to make plans for her children's safety. Her youngest child, Elizabeth, she placed in the care of a household, so that she could be passed off as a child of one of the retainers. The next, Richard, was sent across the sea to Flanders and the eldest, Henry, was sent off with a loyal and trusted shepherd and his wife to a remote part of Cumberland, where the roads were few and travellers rare.

It was there among the fells that the boy grew up as a shepherd lad, living simply, observing the seasons and the stars, and acquiring much rural wisdom. Meanwhile, almost unknown to him, political fortunes turned again. Henry was called from the pastures of Cumberland to take possession of the family home, and once more the banner of the Cliffords floated in the breeze over Skipton Castle. Legend tells us he was not happy in the transformation. The crude splendour of the castle and court was not to his liking. So the "Shepherd Lord" as he was called, retired whenever possible to the Forest of Barden, where he built a lodge now known as Barden Tower. There he discussed astronomy and the theories he had formed in his lonely watches on the Cumberland fells, with the monks of Bolton close by. Even here, however, the calls of politics and affairs of State reached him, and like his predecessors he went forth to do battle. In the year 1513 at the age of 60 he held a command at Flodden Field and acquitted himself well:

From Penighent to Pendle Hill,
From Linton to Long Addingham,
And all that Craven coats did till
They with the lusty Clifford came.

Lady Clifford died at Londesborough in the year 1491 and was there buried near the alter of the church. The "Shepherd Lord" survived Flodden and lived until his seventieth year and his remains lie with those of his ancestors in the peaceful church at Bolton, not far from his quiet retreat at Barden.

THE BOOK OF FATE

IN a tiny deserted cobbler's shop which lay in the very shadows of York Minster a woebegone man was sobbing bitterly and loudly, so loudly in fact that a worthy knight who was passing stopped his horse by the door of the shop and enquired the reason for the tears. "Alack," said the man gloomily, "may Providence forgive me, but I have already five children and know not how to provide for them, and now by wife has just given birth to another daughter."

The knight proved sympathetic and, having some ability as a seer, drew his Book of Fate from his saddle bow and declared he would foretell the child's future. Great was the astonishment of the poor cobbler when the knight grew plainly agitated at what he saw in the book, and still greater was his amazement when the knight turned to him and offered to adopt the newly-arrived infant as his own, promising to make the child heir to his possessions. Sorely distressed at this turn of events but thinking of no better answer, the cobbler consented, and in few moments the knight was cantering away, the strange burden of a newly-born child under his arm. Not until he was out of sight of the city did he stop, and as he rode he turned over in his mind the prophecy of his book that this child was destined to marry his only son.

This he determined with many oaths should not happen, and he spurred his horse till he came to a deserted place by the bank of the river Ouse. Here he dismounted and flung the infant into the middle of the river and with a last oath rode away, rejoicing that he had triumphed over the plans of destiny. Had he stayed a little longer he might have seen the helpless little bundle washed up on the shore and watched its discovery by an old fisherman who bore it away tenderly to his cottage.

Some 15 years later the knight was riding with some friends along the banks of the Ouse when they were attracted by a beautiful girl who stood at the door of a fisherman's cottage. They stopped to purchase some fish, and as they bought they marvelled at the graciousness and sweetness of the maid. Even as they rode away they could not forbear to discuss her charms, and as a contribution to the discussion the old knight said that he would look in his Book of Fate to see which of his love-sick friends would marry the maiden. But he did not tell them the result of his consultation with the book for he realized that here was the child he had flung into the stream long before, and that his own son was still destined to be the husband of this girl.

Once more he attempted to prevent the workings of the Book of Fate. Sending to the cottage for the old fisherman who was acting as the girl's guardian, the knight urged that he allow the girl to carry a message from him to his brother, who was a noble knight living in Scarborough. And after some persuasion the fisherman agreed. It was not long before the girl was on her way, bearing in her purse the message of the knight and with a goodly sum of money to assist her on the road. After travelling many miles she came to an inn where she was provided with a room and a comfortable bed on which she soon fell into a sound sleep after the weariness of her journey. Now it chanced that a thief prowled round the inn that night and eventually found access to the room where the girl slept. Her purse lay on the table and as the thief emptied it he discovered the sealed message: "Dear brother – the bearer of this note is a doer of mischief. Put her to death immediately."

Whether it was a rush of compassion on the part of the thief, or the thought that one good turn deserved another, will never be known, but the fact remains that he altered the note to read: "Dear brother – the bearer of this note has all the virtues. Marry her to my son." Next day the girl arose early and continued her journey to Scarborough. When the knight had read the note he presented the maiden to his nephew and the two fell in love at first sight. The news of the wedding, however, reached the bridegroom's father and he set off for Scarborough in great rage to seek an explanation. As he rode into the town he met his daughter-in-law and repeated his exploit of many years before by carrying her off to a lonely place on the seashore. Here he would have killed her had she not begged so hard for mercy and promised to obey any command.

Relenting, he took a gold ring from her finger, flung it out to the waves and made the girl swear that until she saw the ring again and placed it on her finger she would neither see him nor his son. And he left her weeping bitterly, not knowing how to earn a living in that desolate part of the country. As she wandered weary and hungry down the lanes that led away from the sea, she met the retainer of a nobleman's house who was in great trouble because the cook had been taken ill and there was no one to fill the place. The girl volunteered and soon found that she was a favourite of all at the castle. A few weeks later a great banquet was given by the nobleman and many guests were invited. As she looked through the castle window to see the flowing garments and the gay clothes of the men, the new cooking maid – still sorrowful at heart – was astonished to see the knight and his son arrive.

While she was torn between joy and misery she chanced to cut open a fish that was to be prepared for the table and she noticed something sparkle inside its body. It was the knight's ring, thus restored to the very castle where the knight was staying. When the feast was over, as was the custom in those days, the cooking maids and chief servants were called to the banqueting hall and praised for their dishes. It was then that the nobleman pointed out the strange girl who had come to take the place of the indisposed cook. No sooner had the knight set eyes on her than he drew his sword, rushed at her and would have killed her had she not raised her hand on which was the sparkling ring. After the failure of the third attempt to thwart the Book of Fate, the knight acknowledged that he could no longer battle against the course of destiny. He gave the young couple his blessing, and in the best phrase of all fairy stories "they lived happily ever after".

MOTHER, NURSE AND CHILD

OVER a century ago, in 1869, a reputable clergyman wrote to Mr. Baring-Gould to tell him of an odd apparition which appeared at Trinity Church, Micklegate, York.

The clergyman had attended a service at the church one August Sunday morning and sat in the gallery facing the east window, which was of stained glass except for a border of unstained glass all round the window. Before the service began, and then many times during the morning, ghostly figures outside the church moved across the window. They appeared to be two women and a child. One, presumably the mother, came first and then beckoned to the others. The child accompanied by the other woman, possibly the child's nurse, then appeared, and the mother caressed it, seemed greatly distressed, made frantic gestures of despair, and eventually all three figures moved away. This apparition was apparently seen at various times by many people, sometimes vaguely through the stained glass and at other times clearly through the clear glass border. Usually the women were in white, with the features veiled. One account said that the mother's grief was intensified when a hymn was played loudly on the organ. Sunday school children who sat in the gallery were so familiar with the figures that they referred to them as "Mother, nurse and child".

There was nothing in the graveyard outside the church to create the strange drama. Indeed one rector who wanted to get rid of the apparition notion had some trees felled so that their reflection on the glass could not create an illusion of figures. But the apparitions continued to appear. So the legend grew that they were the ghosts of a York family – father, mother and only child – who had lived nearby many years before. When the plague broke out in the city it carried off the child and, as was the custom, its body was buried outside the city walls to avoid the spread of infection. The child's parents were buried in a grave in the churchyard near the east window. So the ghostly nurse brought the child back from its plague pit to the grave of its parents to the mingled joy and distress of the mother.

JOVIAL ARCHBISHOP

ONE of the merriest archbishops of York was surely Henry Bowett, the 49th holder of the office, who was translated from the Bishopric of Bath and Wells in 1405 and died in 1423. He preferred his palace at Otley to that at York, and claret to any other drink. He was reputed to consume with congenial friends fourscore tuns of claret each year (a tun was 252 wine gallons) and one of his earliest tasks was to enlarge the palace kitchens. Of him, or someone very like him, a poet wrote:

The poet Praed's immortal Vicar
Who wisely wore the cleric gown;
Sound in theology and in liquor
Quite human, though a true divine.
His fellow men he would not libel
He gave his friends good, honest wine
And drew his doctrine from the Bible.

The tomb of this jovial man is seen in York Minster.

POETIC LANDLORD

ALEXANDER Mackintosh was landlord of the *Red Lion Inn* at Driffield, a sportsman, and a poet. His hostelry was famed as a meeting place for owners of greyhounds and other dogs, for anglers and for those interested in "hunting, hawking, coursing and other field sports". He wrote a book, published in 1810, entitled *The Driffield Angler*, which included instructions on shooting, the manner of killing deer and the training of greyhounds, and it ran to several editions. In it he immortalised Snowball, a greyhound of legendary fame, owned by a certain major of Topham.

> *The outstretched Wolds where glory won,*
> *In many a nobler course, her speed*
> *Snowball resigns unto her breed*
> *Hung around with trophies of her praise*
> *The prizes of her youthful days.*

He also recorded in his book two almost legendary pike, one caught at Driffield weighing 28lb. and another at Rise weighing 38lb.

SANCTUARY AT BEVERLEY

THE right of sanctuary from private revenge or the severities of the law has been recognised from the very earliest times. In Biblical records there is evidence of the existence of cities of refuge. Greeks and Romans alike had their sacred places where the fugitive could find at least a temporary respite from his pursuers. Very early in Christian history the custom of allowing Christian churches to offer protection to those fleeing from justice came into existence, and an important part of the duty of the clergy was that of acting as intermediaries between criminals and the officers of justice.

Under a code of laws drawn up by Alfred the Great, church "rith" or sanctuary was recognised, and sanctuary seekers were protected for seven days, or under certain circumstances for 30 days. Occasionally it happened that the sanctuary right was violated, and the penalty for such violation was very severe. The most notable case of sacrilege of this sort was, of course, the murder of Thomas a' Becket at the Altar of St. Benedict in his own cathedral church of Canterbury. Among the oldest and most important of all the sanctuary rights throughout the kingdom were those pertaining to Beverley and its Minster.

In honour of St. John of Beverley privileges were granted by King Athelstan in the year 937 and continued for over 500 years. By these the rights of sanctuary existed in the distance of one league, or about a mile and a half from the Minster in every direction. Within this great sanctuary circle were other boundaries coming closer to the Minster. The third of these began at the entrance to the churchyard, the fourth at the nave door, and the fifth at the choir screen, and the sixth and last at the actual high altar and Frith Stool which stood close by. For violating these various bounds the penalties were incresingly great as they approached the Minster, varying from a fine of eight pounds at the outer boundary to the forfeit of life for any sacrilege at the high altar.

How strong was the general belief in the "divine rights of sanctuary" is shown in a story told by Alfred, a priest of the Minster, in the reign of Henry I: At the time when William the Conqueror was "wasting the North" in revenge for rebellion against his rule, his troops were stationed near Beverley and as a result the local people fled to the church for protection. Some of the soldiers decided to raid the church for plunder, and led by one Toustain on horseback they entered the church. But no sooner had Toustain crossed the threshold than his horse stumbled, and Toustain fell with his neck broken and hands distorted like those of a mis-shapen monster. The soldiers fled in terror at the sight and even the Conqueror was dismayed when told the story, so that he confirmed all the privileges of the church, gave it a grant of lands at Sigglesthorne,

and decreed that the laws of the blessed Saint John should be everywhere spared from the "Wasting".

The Frith Stool was a wide stone chair, once probably inscribed, but now with all traces of lettering defaced. The chair, which may date from the time of Athelstan himself, was the goal of pursued men for many miles around, and if stones could speak it could relate many dramatic stories of those who had committed some grave wrong finding refuge there from the hand of the law or the fury of revengeful relatives. From as far away as Norfolk, Devon, Lancaster, and Cumberland fugitives fled to Beverley, racing against their pursuers, to throw themselves at the mercy of the Church.

Whose who had committed murder, theft or other crimes, on coming within the bounds were received there by officials of the church and allowed to stay for 30 days and nights within the precincts of the Minster. Food and accommodation were provided, and during the time of their stay it was the duty of the canons to endeavour to obtain peace and pardon for the fugitives. If these efforts failed, then at the end of the 30 days the offender was taken to the outer boundary and handed over to the coroner who had then to offer the fugitive the choice of taking his trial or being outlawed from the realm. In the latter case the fugitive was given a fixed time in which to reach a named port from where he was conveyed overseas, never to return.

Beverley, however, had a third alternative – in which it differed from most other ecclesiastical sanctuaries. This was the right of the criminal to take an oath swearing to become a servant of the church and to live within the town of Beverley for the rest of the fugitive's life. Those who accepted this method were known as Frithmen. A Frithman had to surrender to the Crown all his possessions either in land or money, but was allowed to live anywhere within the area of immunity, and to follow his own craft and trade. He could not become a burgess but could hold

office in his trade guild, and there is evidence that many became very prosperous. In common with many other ecclesiastical rights, the special sanctuary privileges of Beverley were swept away by Henry VIII, about 1540, and despite many attempts to restore it the same all-embracing liberty never returned to the church.